From Empathy to Action

How can we move children from simply talking about things to learning to take action – and feeling empowered to enact change? This book shows you exactly what this can look like in an elementary class setting. It details the structures and instructional strategies classroom teachers can adopt to help their children create positive outcomes for their communities while also building identities for themselves as real agents of change.

Topics include building empathy and compassion, helping students become aware of issues within their communities, creating brave environments so students can engage in productive discussions around sensitive topics, engaging students in research that answers their needs and those of their community, and supporting students into action. Classroom examples, practical tools, and student voices are featured throughout.

With this book by your side, you can debunk the false deficit-based assumptions that young people aren't ready for activism, and you'll see what is possible when we commit ourselves to integrating civic learning into our classroom literacy instruction.

Chris Hass is an Assistant Professor in the Department of Early, Elementary, and Reading Education at James Madison University. Previously, he spent 20 years teaching in early childhood and elementary classrooms. His book, *Social Justice Talk*, was published in 2020.

Katie Kelly is a Professor of Education at Furman University and was formerly an elementary classroom teacher and a literacy coach in North Carolina and New York. Katie is widely published in several peer-reviewed journals and books for educators.

Lester Laminack, Professor Emeritus, Western Carolina University in Cullowhee, North Carolina, is a full-time writer and consultant working with schools throughout the United States and abroad. He is the author of over 25 books for teachers and children.

Equity and Social Justice in Education Series
Paul C. Gorski, Series Editor

Routledge's Equity and Social Justice in Education series is a publishing home for books that apply critical and transformative equity and social justice theories to the work of on-the-ground educators. Books in the series describe meaningful solutions to racism, white supremacy, economic injustice, sexism, heterosexism, transphobia, ableism, neoliberalism, and other oppressive conditions that pervade schools and school districts.

Social Studies for a Better World, Second Edition
A Guide for Elementary Educators
Noreen Naseem Rodríguez and Katy Swalwell

Teaching Storytelling in Classrooms and Communities
Amplifying Student Voices and Inspiring Social Change
Maru Gonzalez, Michael Kokozos, and Christy Byrd

Igniting Real Change for Multilingual Learners
Equity and Advocacy in Action
Carly Spina

Anti-Oppressive Universal Design for Teachers
Building Equitable Classrooms
Diana Ma

Integrating Educator Well-Being, Growth, and Evaluation
Four Foundations for Leaders
Lori Cohen and Elizabeth Denevi

Humanizing Pedagogies with Multilingual Learners
Transforming Teaching in Content Areas
Kara Mitchell Viesca and Nancy L. Commins

From Empathy to Action
Empowering K–6 Students to Create Change Through Reading, Writing, and Research
Chris Hass, Katie Kelly, and Lester Laminack

From Empathy to Action

Empowering K–6 Students to Create Change Through Reading, Writing, and Research

Chris Hass, Katie Kelly, and Lester Laminack

Routledge
Taylor & Francis Group
NEW YORK AND LONDON

Designed cover image: © Chris Hass, Katie Kelly, and Lester Laminack

First published 2026
by Routledge
605 Third Avenue, New York, NY 10158

and by Routledge
4 Park Square, Milton Park, Abingdon, Oxon, OX14 4RN

Routledge is an imprint of the Taylor & Francis Group, an informa business

© 2026 Chris Hass, Katie Kelly, and Lester Laminack

The right of Chris Hass, Katie Kelly, and Lester Laminack to be identified as authors of this work has been asserted in accordance with sections 77 and 78 of the Copyright, Designs and Patents Act 1988.

All rights reserved. No part of this book may be reprinted or reproduced or utilised in any form or by any electronic, mechanical, or other means, now known or hereafter invented, including photocopying and recording, or in any information storage or retrieval system, without permission in writing from the publishers.

Trademark notice: Product or corporate names may be trademarks or registered trademarks, and are used only for identification and explanation without intent to infringe.

ISBN: 978-1-032-74589-3 (pbk)
ISBN: 978-1-003-47294-0 (ebk)

DOI: 10.4324/9781003472940

Typeset in ITC Cheltenham
by KnowledgeWorks Global Ltd.

Contents

Acknowledgements vii

Meet the Authors ix

                    Introduction 1

CHAPTER 1 Helping Students Better Understand and Empathize with Others 15

CHAPTER 2 Helping Students Become More Aware of Issues Within the Community 49

CHAPTER 3 Helping Students Engage in Critical Discussion 77

CHAPTER 4 Helping Students Conduct Research 109

CHAPTER 5 Helping Students Take Action 141

                    Conclusion 179

References 187

Acknowledgements

We have been fortunate to collaborate and learn alongside many incredible educators and students who commit themselves to creating a better and more just world for all. In this book, we've drawn from many of their stories to show readers what meaningful action can look like both inside and outside of the classroom. We would like to thank all the students who have contributed their work, their reflections, and their hope for a better world with us so that we could share these with teachers across the country. We would also like to thank educators Katelyn Barnett, Emma Begg, Sarah Brower, Lisa Helsel, Kate Kissam, Nozsa Kyler, Johnna Malici, Rutland Martin, Kevin McArevey, Tianna Myers, Rafa Navarro, Tim O'Keefe, Tiffany Palmatier, Melody Powell, Madison Siekman, Alexa Weeks, and Taylor Wuerfel. Your work continues to inspire us.

Meet the Authors

Chris Hass is an Assistant Professor of Education at James Madison University in Harrisonburg, Virginia. Drawing on his 20 years of experience as a classroom teacher in grades 2–5, Chris conducts research alongside local teacher-partners to explore culturally relevant teaching, the implementation of global learning, critical dialogue, and civic action. He serves on the Executive Board of the Early Childhood Education Assembly and is a column editor for Language Arts where his "Civic Literacy" column supports educators to promote civic engagement in K–5 classrooms.

Chris has worked with teachers in both national and international settings to help them create classroom practices that celebrate the social identities of their students, help learners gain a better understanding and appreciation for diversity, explore issues of inequity and injustice, and support students to take civic and social action. His first book, *Social Justice Talk: Strategies for Teaching Critical Awareness*, was published in 2020.

Katie Kelly is a Professor of Education at Furman University in Greenville, South Carolina. As a former teacher and literacy coach, Katie's teaching and research interests include engaging children in meaningful literacy experiences and practices to foster critically curious and compassionate lifelong readers and writers.

She has widely published in various peer-reviewed journals such as ILA's *The Reading Teacher*. She has co-authored several books including *From Empathy to Action: Empowering K–6 Students to Create Change through Reading, Writing, and Research* (Routledge), *Critical Comprehension: Lessons for Guiding Students to Deeper Meaning* (Corwin); *Reading To Make a Difference: Using Literature to Help Students Think Deeply Speak Freely and Take Action* (Heinemann); *From Pencils to Podcasts: Digital Tools to Transform K–12 Literacy Practices* (Solution Tree); and *Smuggling Writing: Strategies that Get Students to Write Every Day, in Every Content Area* (Corwin).

**Lester Laminack**, Professor Emeritus, Western Carolina University in Cullowhee, North Carolina, is a full-time writer and consultant working with schools throughout the United States and abroad. He is the author or co-author of numerous articles and over 25 books for teachers and children. His academic publications include *Climb Inside a Poem* (Heinemann), *Cracking Open the Author's Craft* (Scholastic), *Bullying Hurts: Teaching Kindness Through Read Aloud and Guided Conversations* (Heinemann), *The Writing Teacher's Troubleshooting Guide* (Heinemann), *Writers ARE Readers: Flipping Reading Strategies into Writing Instruction* (Heinemann), *Reading to Make a Difference* (Heinemann), *The Ultimate Read Aloud Guide* 2nd *Edition* (Scholastic), *The Ultimate Read Aloud Collection Fiction and Nonfiction* (Scholastic), and *Critical Comprehension: Lessons for Guiding Students to Deeper Meaning* (Corwin).

Lester is also the author of several children's books including *The Sunsets of Miss Olivia Wiggins*, *Trevor's Wiggly-Wobbly Tooth*, *Saturdays and Teacakes*, *Jake's 100th Day of School*, *Snow Day!*, *Three Hens and a Peacock* (2012 Children's Choice K–2 Book of the Year Award), *The King of Bees*, *Three Hens and a Peacock*, and *The Enormous Egg*, all published by Peachtree Publishers. His most recent book is *A Cat Like That*.

Lester is available for professional development and school author visits.

Introduction

After reading Linda Sue Park's *A Long Walk to Water,* and discovering Salva Dut's life as a Lost Boy from South Sudan, students in Johnna Malici's fifth-grade class were left with many questions.

Where do all the refugees go?
Why does this happen?
Where else does this happen?

Now aware of a pressing issue and empathetic to the experiences of those affected by displacement, these students were inspired to learn more about refugees from other parts of the world. To support their inquiry, Johnna curated a text set to help them learn about the experiences of people who have been displaced. She included the novel *Refugee* by Alan Gratz and partnered this with picture books such as Margriet Ruurs' *Stepping Stones* and Suzanne Del Rizzo's *My Beautiful Birds*, as well as the poem "Home" by Warsan Shire. Students then worked collaboratively to research countries with high percentages of refugees to find out why refugees were fleeing, how long the problem had been occurring, and where refugees were going. Johnna's students created infographics to teach their peers about the various refugee groups.

Yet, somehow they weren't quite satisfied. Informed with knowledge about the ways some groups were being persecuted around the world, they sought to take action and do something about it. Together, these young advocates brainstormed ways they could take action and decided to host a Refugee Awareness Week at their school. This culminated with the development of a social media post, a series of speeches (see Figure I.1), and a "Walk for Refugees" in the local community. As a result of their efforts, they helped people within the school and surrounding community better understand this ongoing global crisis while also raising over $3,000 for a local nonprofit that supports displaced individuals and families (Laminack & Kelly, 2019).

Johnna's work alongside her students shows us what is possible when the carefully selected texts we use as instructional tools not only teach state

FIGURE I.1

A Fifth-Grade Student Makes a Speech at the Walk for Refugees

standards but also help students become more aware of, and empathetic to, the experiences of people both like and unlike themselves. In selecting such powerful texts that inspired her students to inquire further and eventually take action, Johnna demonstrated how English Language Arts (ELA) teachers can integrate civic literacy into their existing literacy instruction.

> ***Civic literacy*** is defined here as the knowledge that is necessary to participate in democratic processes as well as create positive change within a community. These efforts to create change can occur through political and non-political processes.

With civics education often limited to the social studies classroom, many literacy teachers may not see the connection or receive professional support for such work. This is especially true for those at the elementary level since civic learning is often reserved for a single, one-semester, high school course. Nevertheless, preparation for civic life warrants further exploration across all grade levels and content areas. Civically engaged ELA curriculum that centers on socially relevant themes and current events can foster problem-solving, activism, and agency to change the world (Cervetti & Pearson, 2023). Our aim in writing this book is to demonstrate what civically engaged ELA instruction can look like with younger students as we support them in responsible citizenship. In doing so, we work from the belief that it is the responsibility of all teachers to foster civic engagement in hopes that our students will take charge in creating more just and equitable communities for all.

Civically Engaged Literacy Practices

In his final days, Congressman John Lewis wrote an essay encouraging Americans to fight for democracy. Lewis wrote, "Democracy is not a state. It is an act, and each generation must do its part to help build what we called the Beloved Community, a nation and world society at peace with itself… Now is your turn to let freedom ring" (to hear the essay go to this link: https://www.youtube.com/watch?v=R0LZ6oUYLCc).

Yet, 6 months later on January 6, 2021, a violent mob attacked the U.S. Capitol in Washington D.C. after the defeat of President Trump in the 2020 election. This resulted in five deaths, many injuries, and a further divided nation. False claims that the election was stolen resulted in harm to human life and threatened our democracy. With election deniers, ongoing racial tensions, voter suppression, and increased polarization across our country, civics education is more important than ever. By investing in civic learning, we can strengthen American democracy (Guardian of Democracy: The Civic Mission of Schools report, 2011). As Lewis stated, democracy is an act. And as an act, it is active, not static. It is dynamic, evolving, and changing. It is a work in progress and requires all of us to commit to working collectively toward a more equitable and just future.

As educators, each of us has a responsibility to prepare young people to be critically engaged global citizens. Already, we see examples of what is possible when looking at the powerful work young people such as Thandiwe Abdullah (racial justice), Greta Thurnberg (climate change), Malala Yousafza (access to education), and David Hogg (gun violence) have done to create safer, healthier, and more just communities for all. We can only imagine the collective efforts their teachers made, in support of all they were learning at home, to help them attain the knowledge, skills, and agency that has served them and their communities so well.

For example, in the days after the shooting at Marjorie Stoneman Douglas High School, while David Hogg, X González, and their classmates were speaking with news agencies to plead for safer schools, accusations surfaced that they were not students, but paid crisis actors. (Listen to X González here: https://www.youtube.com/watch?v=u46HzTGVQhg). Many of those in opposition to stricter gun laws were unwilling to accept that these students were so well-informed. Hogg explained that in the days after the shooting at his school, "People couldn't believe that teenagers could be so eloquent or know so much. Right? They literally thought it was more likely that we worked for some government agency trying to take everyone's guns instead of the fact that we could have a public education that actually did its job and prepared and equipped students to lead in moments like that. I had spent years debating issues like 'How do we prevent gun violence?', on both sides". (Listen to the interview with David Hogg here: https://www.npr.org/programs/fresh-air/2023/06/08/1181006641/fresh-air-for-june-8-2023-parkland-school-shooting-survivor-david-hogg)

Mr. Hogg's praise for the work his teachers had done to help him to better understand and engage with the world around him speaks volumes for what is possible in all of our classrooms. In the years since that school shooting, Mr. Hogg has gone on to graduate from Harvard while continuing to advocate for gun safety and youth leadership. When education is committed to cultivating compassionate, civically minded young people, we prepare each new generation to fulfill their potential and contribute to society in meaningful ways.

Democracy and Education

One way we begin to cultivate agentive students such as those mentioned above is to create classroom practices that view education as a liberatory practice. We are defining liberatory practice as an approach to teaching that positions students to collaboratively create new knowledge within a classroom that fosters inclusion and empowerment. To achieve this, we create democratic classrooms built on trusting relationships, shared decision-making, and student-centered participatory learning. We are also careful to spend more time listening, and less time talking so that our students have space to draw upon their funds of knowledge and their genius within (Moll et al., 1992; Muhammad, 2020). Lastly, we center our students' identities, interests, curiosities, and concerns in our teaching so that we can increase their sense of purpose and engagement when learning both in and out of the classroom.

> Funds of knowledge (Moll et al., 1992) refers to the historically accumulated and culturally developed bodies of knowledge and skills that children and their families possess.

Additionally, it's important that we carefully consider the impact our approach to curriculum can have on the civic knowledge and civic identities of our students. Speaking to the relationship between the content we teach and the goals we establish for student learning, Ehrenworth et al. (2020) argue that our aim should be to "create more alert, thoughtful, engaged, inquisitive, and active citizens by reframing teaching so that it's not only about content and standards but also about *civic virtues*" (p. xxiii). They go on to further argue that teachers need to create authentic opportunities where students practice – not memorize – what it means to be a citizen in our democracy.

The idea that classroom learning and civic engagement belong hand-in-hand can be traced as far back as the founding fathers. Within a position statement titled "Revitalizing Civic Learning in Our Schools", The National Council for the Social Studies (NCSS) note that "…Thomas Jefferson, Horace Mann, John Dewey and other great educators understood public schools do not serve a public so much as create a public. The goal of schooling, therefore, is not merely preparation for citizenship, but citizenship itself; to equip a citizenry with the knowledge, skills, and dispositions needed for active and engaged civic life" (Position Statement of National Council for the Social Studies, 2013). At the heart of this work is a belief that our students are not citizens-in-waiting. Rather, with access to knowledge and support, they are already capable of playing an important role within their communities.

It is important to note, however, that visions of a civic education have long been reserved for only a fraction of the population. This commitment to preparing students to play a transformative role in civic life would not have been found in the assimilation boarding schools where, for roughly a century, thousands of Indigenous children were taken from their homes in an effort to strip them of their cultural knowledge and practices. The education offered in these schools was not meant to prepare students to transform their communities but to transform themselves so they could dutifully take their assigned place within a country that actively worked to silence their voices, trample upon their rights, and severely limit their opportunities for social or financial mobility. Furthermore, Black and Brown children were subject to a similar campaign of assimilation after being integrated into public schools alongside their white peers.

Still, in contrast to these unjust systems of education there are powerful examples of literacy learning being used as an opportunity to create needed change. For instance, Black literate societies were created in the 1800s as collaborative teaching and learning spaces where members of the Black community could build knowledge, fight injustice, and advocate for rights (Muhammad, 2020). Black literate societies embraced literacy as an act of liberation and empowerment to counter oppression and racism. Serving as a model of what is possible, these societies offered" emancipatory and humanizing aspects of literacy [to] provide access to mental freedom, political power, and agenda building" (Muhammad, 2020, p. 19). A similar approach was later adopted by the Freedom Schools of the 1960s as they worked to use teaching and learning as a means of connecting learning to the specific social and political needs of their communities.

Developing Curriculum to Meet the Needs of the Community

When we look at our own curriculum, what messages are we sending to our students about the purpose of learning? Is it, as Muhammad suggested, about access to mental freedom, power, and agency building? Or is it about preparation for high-stakes assessments and, eventually, the job market? For more than a century, progressive scholars have challenged educators to consider the role education plays within a society (Counts, 1932; Dewey, 1903; Friere, 2000; Giroux, 1988; Macedo, 2006). They have argued that traditional approaches to curriculum and instruction merely train a future workforce of docile workers (Apple, 2013) who serve as human capital willing to "do the nation's chores without asking too many troublesome questions" (Evans, 2000, p. 298). Mirra and Morrell (2011), contend that this reductive view of teaching and learning focuses on high-stakes accountability, basic skills, passive consumption of knowledge, and education for individual economic gain. Such schooling – favoring standardization and patriotism over civic education, culturally relevant teaching, and critical thought – avoids issues of difference and power while presenting education as a means for individual, personal gain.

High-quality education that integrates civic learning into the existing curriculum helps students address complex problems, work with a diverse group of peers, and engage in creative problem-solving (NCSS, 2013). Civically engaged young people are more likely to vote, be involved in their communities, speak publicly, and communicate with elected officials (Guardian of Democracy: The Civic Mission of Schools report, 2011, p. 6).

> According to the Civic Mission of Schools Report (2003), competent and responsible citizens share four common traits:
> - **Informed and thoughtful.** They have a grasp and an appreciation of history and the fundamental processes of American democracy, an

understanding and awareness of public and community issues, an ability to obtain information when needed, a capacity to think critically, and a willingness to enter into dialogue with others about different points of view and to understand diverse perspectives. They are tolerant of ambiguity and resist simplistic answers to complex questions.

- **Participate in their communities.** They belong to and contribute to groups in civil society that offer venues for Americans to participate in public service; work together to overcome problems; and pursue an array of cultural, social, political, and religious interests and beliefs.
- **Act politically.** They have the skills, knowledge, and commitment needed to accomplish public purposes – for instance, by organizing people to address social issues, solving problems in groups, speaking in public, petitioning and protesting to influence public policy, and voting.
- **Moral and civic virtues.** They are concerned for the rights and welfare of others, socially responsible, willing to listen to alternative perspectives, confident in their capacity to make a difference, and ready to contribute personally to civic and political action. They strike a reasonable balance between their own interests and the common good. They recognize the importance of and practice civic duties such as voting and respecting the rule of law.

Student-Centered Learning

A civically engaged classroom, therefore, requires a shift from traditional models of education that have long positioned teachers as authority figures who dispense knowledge to students, as though they are empty vessels. Positioning teachers as transmitters of knowledge is dehumanizing and impedes the development of critical comprehension and civic skills. Freire (2000) refers to this as the banking method of education and argues for a more reciprocal approach in a democratic environment where students and teachers learn together through dialogue. Children are not passive beings. It is not in their nature to simply sit and receive. Watch children at play, they are active and engaged, they negotiate rules and limits, they challenge what they perceive as "unfair" and work through the problems to sustain their play.

In this book, we advocate for instruction that flows with the nature of the child. A student-centered classroom transfers power from the teacher and positions students as knowledgeable, curious, and capable learners who co-create learning experiences alongside the teacher and their peers. When students are actively engaged in learning and are agents of the learning experience, instruction will be more effective and students will become critically empowered civic agents who work collectively for change. The approach builds on the language and knowledge that students bring to the curriculum. Teachers listen to the questions, concerns, insights, and (mis)understandings of students as they guide them to resources and processes that will allow them to work collaboratively to gain greater insight and deeper understanding.

Laying the Groundwork for a Civically Engaged Classroom

To begin this work in the classroom, we recommend building a solid foundation by co-constructing class agreements to guide students' learning, discussions, decisions, and actions. To ensure all voices are heard, valued, and respected in democratic learning environments, classroom agreements center the community's values and goals. We suggest starting this work at the beginning of the school year by bringing the class together to share the hopes, goals, and expectations they have for themselves and their peers as a community of learners. These agreements should be fluid as the community evolves, constantly reflecting on what is working, what is a struggle, and what changes need to occur. By collaboratively constructing these norms and revisiting them regularly, we find that individuals grow and change over weeks and months, as does the community.

We do this same work with older learners. For instance, In one of Katie's college-level education classes, she read the children's book, *Our Class is a Family* by Shannon Olsen. The book served as a springboard for a classroom conversation to collaboratively create classroom norms. This shared experience served as an example of how a similar approach could be used in the students' future elementary-level classrooms. Katie explained that the goal is to create a learning environment where everyone feels safe to be themselves, share openly, and push one another to consider new knowledge, experiences, and perspectives. She then modeled an example of a proactive, positive statement to contribute to the class agreements chart (e.g. "We actively listen and seek to understand even when our views may differ"). Next, she invited students to brainstorm additional agreements they believe are important to foster a productive, inclusive, democratic learning environment. These agreements were referred to regularly throughout the school year and were revisited and revised as necessary (see Figure I.2). Creating classroom agreements helps lay the foundation for a supportive classroom culture filled with care and respect,

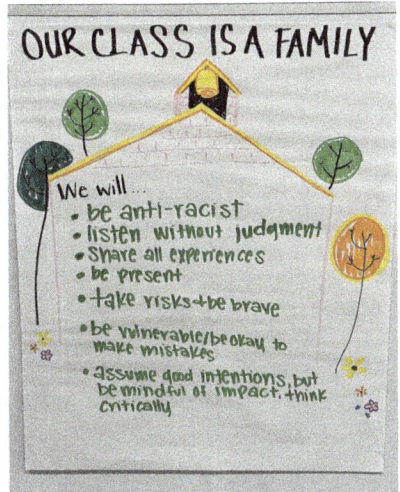

FIGURE I.2

Sample of a Norms Anchor Chart

which Ehrenworth et al. (2020) identify as a key condition for creating a civically engaged classroom.

In addition to collaboratively constructing classroom norms, we must also work intentionally to nurture the skills and habits necessary to engage critically with a variety of texts, ideas, events, and others. By reading critically from multiple perspectives, readers make more informed decisions about what information to take away, what information to question, and what information to leave behind (Janks, 2014; Kelly et al., 2023). Reading, viewing, and listening to the world from multiple perspectives allows students to expand their understandings, perceptions, and assumptions. It leads to awareness of power and privilege, oppression and injustice, hope and liberation. It fosters critical curiosity and a desire to learn more about local issues and activism. Civically engaged classrooms promote hope and belief in the ability to change systems, expose oppression, and influence others (Ehrenworth et al., 2020, p. xxv).

The Guardian of Democracy: The Civic Mission of Schools Report identifies six proven practices that constitute a well-rounded high-quality civic learning experience:

- **Classroom Instruction**: Schools should provide direct instruction in government, history, economics, law, and democracy in ways that provoke analysis and critical thinking skills. These subjects are vital to laying the foundation for civic learning and may also contribute to young people's tendency to engage in civic and political activities over the long term. However, schools should avoid teaching only rote facts about dry procedures, which is unlikely to benefit students and may actually alienate them from politics.

- **Discussion of Current Events and Controversial Issues:** Schools should incorporate discussion of current local, national, and international issues and events into the classroom, particularly those that young people view as important to their lives. Engaging students in civil dialogue about controversial issues provides opportunities to foster character and civic virtue – important civic dispositions that are the habits of the heart and mind conducive to the healthy functioning of the democratic system. Examples include civility, open-mindedness, compromise, and toleration of diversity, all of which are prerequisites of a civic life in which the American people can work out the meanings of their democratic principles and values.

- **Service-Learning**: Schools should provide students with relevant and motivational opportunities to connect formal classroom instruction with the principles and processes of democratic life through practical community problem-solving. With guided practice in collaborative problem-solving through public policy approaches, students learn to make long-term differences that will be sustained over time. They learn firsthand about the advantages of working as a group, the influence of public policy on human lives, and the intricacies of local government and community politics. They also develop firsthand knowledge of such abstract concepts as justice, diversity, opportunity, equality, and the common good, while developing empathy and compassion for others. Most importantly, students learn that American society is "unfinished" and that they can play a key role in narrowing the disparity between our democratic ideals and the reality of daily life by registering to vote, voting in elections, and influencing public policy.

- **Extracurricular Activities**: Schools should provide opportunities for young people to get involved in their schools or communities outside of the classroom. Extracurricular activities provide forums for students to practice civic skills and knowledge in purposeful ways while building important collaboration and communication skills. Civic activities such as mock trials, model congress, speech and debate, and model U.N. all have positive impacts on students' civic knowledge and engagement. Students who participate in these types of extracurricular activities are more likely to remain civically engaged well beyond high school.

- **School Governance:** Schools should encourage student participation in school governance. Effective student governments serve a number of important purposes in our schools. They are laboratories in which students can learn and practice essential citizenship skills, respect for human dignity, and the value of the democratic process. They provide students with effective forums for advocating new ideas and initiating school improvements. Effective student governments also provide a platform for the orderly expression of conflicting viewpoints and procedures for resolving conflicts when students disagree with policies and decisions that affect their lives.

- **Simulations of Democratic Processes:** Schools should encourage students to participate in simulations of democratic processes and procedures. Simulations of voting, trials, legislative deliberation, and diplomacy in schools can lead to heightened political knowledge and interest. Students learn skills with clear applicability to both civic and non-civic contexts, such as public speaking, teamwork, close reading, analytical thinking, and the ability to argue both sides of a topic. All of these are skills that prepare students both for active citizenship and for future academic and career success.

Activism and Advocacy: Are They the Same Thing?

Activism and advocacy are similar in several important ways. First, both aim to draw attention to a particular issue. When Malala Yousafzai spoke to the United Nations about the troubling state of educational opportunity (advocacy), she brought attention to the lack of access many children across the globe have to formal and quality schooling. Similarly, when, in 1960, Black students from North Carolina A&T sat at the lunch counter of a segregated Woolworth's store in Greensboro, North Carolina (activism), they forced their community, and the nation-at-large, to continue debating the persistence of Jim Crow laws that had been bolstered by Plessy vs Ferguson more than a half-century before.

Secondly, both activism and advocacy aim to influence the decision-making process of targeted groups such as community members, voters, elected officials, CEOs, and government agencies to support and initiate needed change. For instance, Malala not only delivered a speech that was shared with the world she also publicly placed specific demands on global leaders to provide an education for every child. In the case of the Greensboro sit-in, the attention these students' forceful actions brought to segregation placed social, political, and financial pressure on segregated businesses and officials across the South.

Yet, there are some important distinctions between these two terms that need to be explored.

Advocacy is about trying to persuade others, shift attitudes, or garner broader favor for a particular set of values or needed actions (McKeever et al., 2023). Student examples of advocacy include writing a letter to the school board about their negative experiences with excessive testing, inviting a state senator into the classroom to learn about their needs concerning better school funding, creating informational posters to convince the student body to reduce trash by recycling and composting, and giving a formal presentation at an assembly to teach other classes about the whitewashing of history found in their textbooks while calling on other classes to diversify the texts and historical perspectives they access in their own learning.

Activism, on the other hand, often takes the form of direct, vigorous action that is designed to exert pressure on a targeted person or group of people in an attempt to challenge an existing condition, practice, or policy (Lewis,

2018; McKeever et al., 2023; Ophelie, 2016). Student examples of activism include organizing or participating in: a Black Lives Matter march, a walk-out in response to adopted book bans, a sit-in to demand a plan to reduce gun violence, a protest of police violence against communities of Color that includes kneeling or remaining seated during the Pledge of Allegiance or a boycott of school lunches to pressure district officials to provide a better quality of options.

In this book, we will provide examples of students engaged in both advocacy and activism. Both are integral to creating a more civic-minded and action-oriented citizenry, as well as creating more just communities for all.

What to Expect from This Book

So much is possible when we come to recognize the power and potential of using literacy learning as a vehicle for civic learning and social change. When Johnna chose to read *A Long Walk to Water* and responded to the tensions this story created for her students, she created an authentic opportunity for everyone in that classroom, including herself, to engage with the world in a more intentional, humane, and responsible manner. Her fifth graders were inspired by their reading and research to take action by raising awareness and securing financial support for an organization that actively supports refugees. In doing so, Johnna engaged them in a process (learning about issues that affect a community, conducting research, and then identifying and implementing meaningful action) that influenced these young people as civic learners. The following year, after they had moved on to a nearby middle school, a handful of the students returned to visit Johnna's classroom and informed her that the shared experience in her classroom continued to inspire them to think critically about the world around them and to look for opportunities to create change (Laminack & Kelly, 2019).

In this book, we detail how educators can support students in this vital work. In Chapter 1, we explore ways to help students develop empathy and compassion. Using books not just as windows and doors (Bishop, 1990) but as an opportunity to feel connected to other people and to public life (Mirra, 2018), this chapter examines how to help young people move from empathy to compassion to be more action-oriented in their support for each other while fostering greater equity in their lives and the lives of other people in and out of the classroom.

In Chapter 2, we describe ways educators can help their students become more aware of the issues facing their classroom, schools, community, and world. From powerful read-alouds to current news to classroom visitors, we demonstrate how children of all ages can be introduced to important issues in developmentally appropriate ways.

In Chapter 3, we look at the role of building critical discussions within the classroom where everyone is invited to be part of the collaborative process of creating new meaning – even when it means disagreeing. To get us here, we will show how classroom teachers can work in deliberate ways to create brave environments where students learn to engage in productive discussion around sensitive topics.

In Chapter 4, we demonstrate how to engage students in research that grows out of their own interests and questions, as well as the needs of the community. In doing so, we help students learn the role research plays in developing the background knowledge that is necessary to become informed citizens who are able to take action.

In Chapter 5 we bring everything together to detail how classrooms can move from merely talking and learning about issues to taking action. From whole-class activism projects to scaffolding students into individual projects of their own, we draw on powerful examples to show what is possible when we commit ourselves to integrating civic learning into our classroom literacy instruction.

Finally, in the conclusion we answer questions teachers often ask in light of the political climate facing educators today.

CHAPTER 1

Helping Students Better Understand and Empathize with Others

From the first day Katie met Kamden on one of her visits to Sarah Brower's fourth-grade classroom, he was unforgettable. Struggling to sit still, Kamden was in constant motion while regularly interrupting his teacher and classmates. He introduced himself to Katie and immediately informed her of his attention-deficit/hyperactivity disorder (ADHD) diagnosis, describing it as his superpower. Kamden explained that because he is so social, he enjoys working with his peers. In fact, he and two of his classmates were coauthoring comic books together. Kamden explained that his role in the partnership was valuable because when his coauthors tired, his ADHD helped him step in and continue the work.

Kamden was very aware of his diagnosis and openly discussed his needs. During their opinion writing unit, Kamden focused his writing on the need to provide more support for students with ADHD. Specifically, he advocated that students should be able to chew gum, listen to music when working, and use kick bands (Figure 1.1).

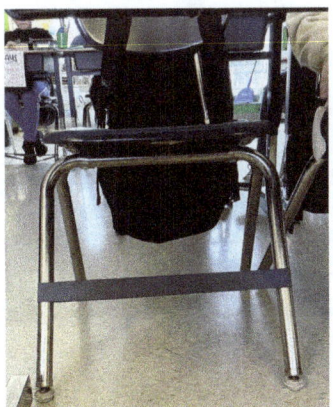

FIGURE 1.1
Kick Band on Kamden's Chair

Voices from the Classroom

Kamden, fourth grader

"I wrote my letter because I felt like it was unfair that kids without ADHD would sit there and be fine but for me [and the principal] we have to sit there holding our patience together when we can blow at any minute and get yelled at even though we have no control over it. So I thought it was unfair and certain things can help deal with that. Like kickbands can help kids with ADHD keep all that energy going without letting it out in different ways so it doesn't distract anyone and they can still learn and let their energy out. I learned that advocating for yourself and for others shows how you are a brave person and not afraid to tell others your words and what you think".

Kamden shared his opinion writing with the school principal. She empathized with his challenges and shared about her own ADHD diagnosis. She was so moved by Kamden's passion and commitment to his cause that she purchased gum for the class to conduct an experiment to determine if it increased their attention. Based on the positive results, the principal permitted gum chewing in the class. Not only did Kamden's writing produce greater empathy and compassion for change, but it increased his interest and engagement in the act of writing. As his teacher noted, "Kamden really struggled to write and never wanted to write anything. He did not identify as a writer. However, by engaging in purposeful writing focused on a topic of his choice, Kamden's passion increased his engagement and the quality of his writing. This really served as an outlet for him to write and grow as a writer which resulted in an attitude change too!"

ADHD Solutions in School!

By Kamden

Kids with ADHD (attention-deficit/hyperactivity disorder) have trouble focusing in class and trying not to move around. In my opinion, I think we should have gum in school because kids like this need something to take out the energy in their bodies. Here is some evidence to prove my point, [our school] has a handbook that says this "Chewing gum is not permitted on the school grounds or in the school building". After hearing

> that in my opinion that rule is unfair to kids with ADHD. I also think that they should be able to listen to music to calm them down when they are having stress during a test or something for a grade that's why it could help them. Here is another thing to prove my point a school in California called California State University-Northridge said when our students listen to music especially the kids with ADHD the reason why is that it calms them down during a test and takes the stress out of them and they feel ok. I also think that they should have flexible sitting in classes so that they have something to move around in when they are bored. Here is my last piece of evidence for you – a school in California lets their students sit in flexible because scientists have discovered that flexible sitting helps them focus in class so that they can learn in a way that is comfortable to them and the reason I am saying all of this is because I'm one of those kids with ADHD and I know we need this because it helps us calm us down during stress and when we don't know what to do when we are bored and we have a lot of energy in our body that can be taken away from us with all of this stuff and I hope that this inspired you because I know it inspired me.

By providing students with opportunities to openly share their experiences, passions, and needs, as Kamden did when advocating for a more ADHD-responsive classroom, we help students come to know their peers better, build greater empathy, and develop stronger connections. To be inspired to take action as a form of advocacy and activism involves compassion which sprouts from seeds of empathy. Before we begin thinking about what it looks like to build empathy that guides our students into action, let's take a moment to explore the differences between sympathy, empathy, and compassion.

Sympathy–Empathy–Compassion

Let's explore the nuances between sympathy, empathy, and compassion. Empathy differs from sympathy and compassion in subtle but critical ways. Empathy is the ability to connect with people to understand and share their thoughts, feelings, and experiences (Bazalgette, 2017; Henshon, 2019). Often used synonymously, sympathy

PAUSE AND REFLECT

Record your own definition of empathy. Consider how it differs from sympathy and compassion. Revisit it after reading this section.

is feeling sorry for someone. It involves understanding what someone is experiencing but through your own perspective, often resulting in pity. Sympathy says, "I'm sorry" whereas empathy says, "I'm hurting with you". "Empathy helps us imagine the pain, joy, suffering, exhilaration, and love that other people feel, informing our choices and leading us to make connections" (Henshon, 2019, p. 14). For example, if a child loses their favorite pencil, a sympathetic response might be, "I'm sorry you lost your pencil, but you need to find something to write with", whereas an empathetic response could sound something like, "I'm sorry you lost your favorite pencil. I know how special it was to you since it has your name on it".

When educators serve as empathetic models, we can foster a sense of belonging in the classroom by creating spaces and structures to support the individual where their feelings are recognized and where they are heard and better understood. It is also important to create opportunities for students to practice and to develop their own empathy skills to help them build connections with their classmates and people they encounter both in and out of the school setting.

PAUSE AND REFLECT

In the margin, write about a time when you experienced empathy (either as the giver or receiver). What happened? How did you feel? How did it impact the other person?

Empathy is a learned behavior that begins in infancy. At around 2 months old, babies begin to develop awareness of other peoples. They react with smiles and coos. Between 9 and 11 months old, babies reach for caregivers and familiar people in their lives. They share moments of pleasure, happiness, or distress. For example, they may cry if they hear other babies in distress. When an infant points to something, they are inviting us to join in the experience together. For instance, when Katie's 20-month-old great-nephew, Morgan, saw an actor slip and fall on the icy steps on T.V., he immediately pointed and announced, "Oh no! He fall!" Shortly before age two, children become aware of themselves by recognizing their faces in the mirror. From here, they begin to develop an awareness of others (Lumbroso, 2015). When visiting a dinosaur exhibit, Morgan offered his pear to the life-size baby dinosaur (Figure 1.2). Over time, children shift from egocentric perspectives as they begin to consider different perspectives. We contend that there is a natural tendency toward empathy when nurtured by social interactions and models of empathy. They shift from perceiving other people's distress to being concerned about their feelings, to understanding these feelings, and to ultimately sharing these feelings or empathizing with them (de Waal, 2008).

FIGURE 1.2

Morgan Shares His Pear

Empathy helps us see the world from multiple viewpoints and experience the world at a deeper level (Henshon, 2019). Empathy includes four qualities. These include the ability to:

- consider multiple perspectives,
- listen without judgment,
- recognize people's emotions
- communicate those emotions (Brown, 2021; Mindshift, 2017).

These are important life skills that can be learned. Below we provide some suggestions and opportunities to practice empathetic speaking and listening skills for learners of all ages.

Empathetic Speaking and Listening

Listening with empathy is about recognizing and centering the other person's feelings without judgment. When responding empathetically to someone else, we want to avoid comparison with ourselves. Statements such as "me too" or "that happened to me" take away the focus from their experience. For example, when Darius shared about feeling sad after his dog was hit by a car and his classmate interrupted to say, "my dog ran away last year", Darius does not receive acknowledgment for being vulnerable to open up and share nor the comfort to help him grieve his loss. Additionally, empathetic responses shouldn't begin with statements such as "at least …". This type of comparison, or silver lining, minimizes the individual's suffering. We also want to avoid attempting to solve the situation by telling the person what to do (e.g. "you should …"). By offering suggestions, the focus shifts from the person's feelings to the problem itself.

Statements	Impact
"That happened to me too".	Shifts focus away from the individual's experience.
"At least …"	Minimizes an individual's suffering.
"You should …"	Shifts focus away from the individual's feelings to the problem.

To be empathetic, we must acknowledge and validate the feelings of those around us. When Darius shared with the class that his dog was hit by a car, a simple acknowledgment of how hard that must be, saying something like "I'm sorry for your loss", or making sympathy cards are ways to demonstrate empathy. Additionally, the teacher or classmates could ask Darius what would help him feel better. Would he like a hug? Does he want to talk about it further? Would it be helpful to read books about loss and grieving or is it too soon? Alternatively, maybe he wants to be distracted with some good jokes to cheer him up.

In other instances where it may not be clear why a student is upset it could be helpful to ask "what" questions to inquire without judgment. For example, in another classroom, Kandace stormed in from recess and immediately put her head down on her desk. In this case, the teacher decided to quietly talk to the student privately to ask her what was wrong and whether or not she wanted to talk about it. Kandace shared that she felt frustrated because it was time to go back to class and she never got a turn to jump double-Dutch. The teacher acknowledged that she understood how that would result in feeling frustrated. Rather than giving her a solution or advice, the teacher then asked Kandace if she had some suggestions for how to change this situation in the future or if she might want to have a class meeting to discuss it and brainstorm ideas together as a class. Kandace agreed that it might be good to have a class meeting to discuss ways to ensure more equitable play time during recess.

Using the guidance in the table below, consider how you would respond to a child who starts crying during independent reading or a child who appears to be sitting alone at the lunch table or another situation that could benefit from an empathetic response.

Action	Statements	Impact
Ask nonjudgemental questions	"What happened that made you feel that way?" "Do you want to talk about what happened?"	Seek to understand without judgment
Restate what you heard	"It sounds like you feel …"	Clarify your understanding and acknowledge the individual's feelings
Ask questions to support next steps	"What might you do now?" "What are you thinking now?" "Is there something I/we/you can do to help with this situation?"	Allow the individual to consider their options
Ask before offering advice	"Would you like me to share my thoughts with you?"	Individual remains in control (and it's ok if they prefer not to request or heed your advice)

What Does This Mean for Our Teaching?

To support students in developing their empathetic speaking and listening skills, provide opportunities for practice. You might begin by reading the picture book, *The Rabbit Listened* by Cori Doerrfeld. In the story, Taylor is sad when the block tower he worked so hard to build is knocked down. Several animals come by and offer Taylor advice but it's only the rabbit who sits quietly and listens to Taylor which is exactly what he needed. After retelling the story together as a class, encourage students to compare how the rabbit's approach differed from the animals in the story. Then ask them to explore how the responses made Taylor feel and why. Explain how sometimes we need to simply be present and listen to offer support.

During a conversation with a friend, Katie recounted a scary situation where a large, unleashed dog charged after her and her small dog during a walk. Rather than responding by saying something like "Oh, that sounds so scary. I'm glad you are both alright" the person explained that it was likely the owner's fault and not the dog's fault. This left Katie feeling frustrated since the dog's behavior was aggressive and resulted in her running with her small dog to escape. Rather than discounting her feelings, Katie just wanted to be heard. Consider something that was difficult for you recently. How would you want someone to respond?

To practice these skills in your classroom, pair students and designate partner A and partner B and assign one partner (e.g. partner A, the person whose name comes first alphabetically, etc.) to share first. Ask them to share an example of something that has been hard for them lately. This can be something in school, in an after-school activity (e.g. sports or a club), at home, or in the larger context of the world around them. It might be something simple like spilling milk at breakfast. Partner B will listen empathetically as partner A shares their story. Provide prompts such as the following to guide partner responses:

- That's awful.
- That sounds challenging.
- Ask "what" questions. (e.g. "What happened that made you feel that way?")
- It sounds like you feel ….
- What do you see as your options?
- What might you want to do about this?
- Would you like for me to share my thoughts with you?

How else can we help students feel more connected? Consider this example of fourth-grade teacher Katelyn Barnett. When she learned that a student's recent absences were due to their family's current experience with homelessness, she considered how to help ease the student's transition when they returned to school. She anticipated that the class might wonder why their classmate had been absent and may bombard them with a flurry of questions making it potentially difficult for the child upon their return to school. While Katelyn never disclosed the child's circumstances, she engaged the class in a discussion of the book, *Just Ask! Be Different, Be Brave, Be You* by Sonia Sotomayor about the differences that make us unique and ways to inquire thoughtfully. Chloe remarked that asking questions can make us feel more connected by learning more about other people. She said, "If you ask questions, you understand more. And you can feel connected by what you understand".

To help students deepen their connection to people, we can use literature as a tool to highlight various situations and ways to respond to them. For instance, Katelyn connected to a previous read-aloud of *Milo Imagines the World* by Matt de la Peña by noting the way Milo, the main character, made initial assumptions about the people he observed on the train. She explained that instead of making assumptions, Milo could've posed nonjudgmental questions such as, "I'm going to visit someone. Where are you going today?". Katelyn explained that just like in the book, we don't always really know what someone else is experiencing and to avoid passing judgment or putting someone in a situation where they may feel uncomfortable, we can be more intentional with our language. In the case of the classmate who has been absent, we don't know why and it may be possible that the child wants to keep that information private. So rather than putting them on the spot with a question like "Where were you?" we can shift to empathetic statements such as, "We missed you!" or "Welcome back!" and more open-ended questions like, "How are you?"

Emotional, Cognitive, and Compassionate Empathy

Empathy is an emotional skill set that allows us to understand what someone is experiencing and communicate that understanding appropriately (Brown, 2021). The three types of empathy include emotional empathy, cognitive empathy, and compassionate empathy. **Emotional empathy** is the capacity to recognize the emotional state of another (e.g. "I see you are sad"). **Cognitive empathy** is the ability to understand the reasons for another person's perspective or feelings (e.g. "I can understand why you're sad because you lost your favorite pencil"). **Compassionate empathy** refers to feeling for another person and taking action on their behalf (e.g. "I can see that you're sad because you lost your pencil. Come on, I'll help you look for it") (Henshon, 2019).

We can plant seeds of empathy to sprout compassion. Compassion is an emotional response to empathy and drives a desire to serve and relieve suffering. According to Goetz et al. (2010), compassion is "the feeling that arises in witnessing another's suffering and that motivates a subsequent desire to help". At its Latin roots, compassion means to "suffer with". In order to take action to relieve suffering (compassionate empathy), we must first engage in emotional and cognitive empathy to be aware of and understand someone's suffering. Sir Ken Robinson described compassion as "applied empathy". He explained, "I think of compassion as ... the executive wing of empathy. It's one thing to empathize with someone's situation, it's something else to do something about it" (2017).

Sympathy	Empathy	Compassion
• Distant • Understand what the person is feeling	• Shared • Feel what a person is feeling	• Connected and action-oriented • Willingness to take action in an attempt to relieve the suffering of another

What Does This Mean for Our Teaching?

As Mirra states, "The development of empathy in students (and teachers) should be considered a primary goal of education because it offers an organizing principle for our field grounded in hope, love, and a commitment to a more equitable society" (2018, p. 3). It is important to teach students skills to develop empathy and compassion. Teaching skills to develop students' empathy and compassion should be a part of our daily classroom practice. Not only will this strengthen the classroom community, but it will cultivate a space where students feel a sense of belonging where they can be their truest selves and will more likely be vulnerable to share more openly. The better we know our students, the better we can support their needs academically, socially, and emotionally. These real-world skills are equally important outside of the classroom setting as children encounter different people and situations in their lives.

Teaching empathy is neither an add-on nor an isolated lesson. Rather, it should be naturally woven into our daily practice. Children develop empathy skills when they are surrounded by empathy. Consider ways you can model empathy and compassion for your students through your own words and actions. For example, what do you do when a student is tardy or submits an assignment late? How do you respond when a colleague labels a student as a "troublemaker" or "struggling"? In what ways do you demonstrate compassion for students' home environments? Rather than judging caregivers for not returning calls or not attending school events, how can you consider their full humanity and the situations that may create roadblocks to participate in traditional Eurocentric schooling practices? In what ways can you shift expectations or practices to be more compassionate and supportive of all students and families?

Event	Empathetic Response	Unempathetic Response
Student is tardy.	"I hope everything is ok". "I'm glad you made it".	"You're late". Asking "why are you late" in front of the whole class.
Student submits work late.	"Thank you for submitting your work. Was there anything specific that made it difficult for you to complete the work on time? Is there something I can do to support you with completing your work?"	"This is late". "I don't grade late work". Assigning a grade of zero or taking points off for being late.
Colleague labels a student as a "troublemaker".	"I think we need to be cautious of labeling the student. It is possible that something is going on that is causing the child's behavior".	Silence. Agreement.
A child's parent or caregiver does not show up for parent conference at school.	Consider possible roadblocks that might prevent the family from attending a school conference. Perhaps they had negative school experiences themselves or aren't available at the requested time due to work schedule or lack of transportation.	They don't care.

    Sarah is another example of a teacher who fosters a classroom community rooted in empathy and compassion. As she engages students in standards-based instruction, she encourages students to express their feelings in a variety of contexts including discussions about events in and out of school. She supports

FIGURE 1.3

Reader Response Sentence Stems

students as they connect with their own feelings first to understand what people are experiencing in real life and within the pages of a book. Sarah seamlessly integrates empathy with character study as part of the reading curriculum. Using sentence stems such as "As a reader, I notice …" and "As a reader, I feel …", Sarah helps her fourth graders engage in close reading of the text while reacting to the text empathetically (Figure 1.3).

For instance, when reading Jacqueline Woodson's book, *The Other Side,* students responded, *"I feel sad because both girls look sad and lonely"*, *"My feelings are sad because Black and white people were not allowed to play with each other"*, and *"I think the message is to love someone even if they're different"* (see Figure 1.4). Providing students with opportunities to respond through writing, discussion, and even quietly inside their minds and hearts helps to process a range of emotions and provides the teacher with insight into students' thinking and feelings. This type of emotional empathy serves as a

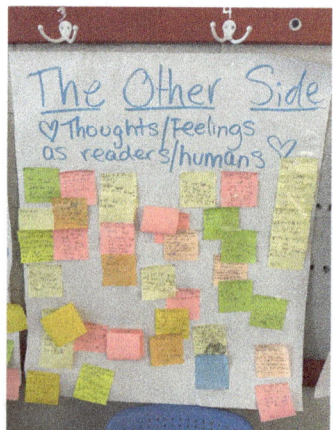

FIGURE 1.4

Student Responses

building block for deeper understanding (cognitive empathy) and taking action (compassionate empathy).

As a reader, I notice …	This makes me feel …	I can be part of the solution by …
Both girls look lonely because they can't go on the other side of the fence.	Sad	Acting as a friend and an ally to anyone who is being mistreated
The girls can't play together because one girl is Black and one is white	Upset	Questioning any rules, laws, or ways of thinking that are meant to keep people apart or privilege one group over another

Reading for Empathy and Compassion

Stories about people similar to us and different from us help us recognize our common humanity, celebrate our differences, and better understand fellow community members (Bazalgette, 2017; Kelly et al., 2023a). As such, literacy and literature hold great power in connecting us as human beings (Mirra, 2018). Studies reveal that reading literary fiction can improve our ability to empathize with (emotional empathy) and understand people's thoughts, feelings, and actions (cognitive empathy).

As readers, we imagine characters' thoughts, feelings, and intentions, and consider how they are similar to or different from our own (Lysaker & Tonge, 2013). With each turn of the page, we interact with the characters and the developing plot. We make connections, build background knowledge, and consider new information as we synthesize successive ideas. We combine information from the text with our prior knowledge and lived experiences to imagine the characters' thoughts, feelings, and motives. This type of inferential thinking is necessary in order for us to engage in perspective taking, a central component of empathy (McCreary & Marchant, 2017). "When the reader stands in [their] own worldview, unable to see or conceive of any other perspective, a book can be a bridge" (Laminack & Kelly, 2019, p. xiii). Stories as bridges provide us with opportunities to witness life from various perspectives moving beyond our lives into the lived experiences of different people.

When exploring perspectives beyond our own, we deepen our understanding of why a person feels the way they do. This level of consciousness and the intellectual work of perspective taking is a form of cognitive empathy. In order to truly engage in compassionate empathy (action), we must move beyond emotional empathy (feeling) toward cognitive empathy (understanding). Carefully selected literature can help us achieve this.

Emotional Empathy and In-Group Bias

Because emotional empathy is strongest among people who identify with one another, it may result in hostility towards members of different groups. For example, Muslim Americans experience discrimination at higher rates. Some women who wear a hijab have been asked why they wear a tablecloth on their head. Multilingual speakers have been told to speak English (despite there not being a national language in the U.S.) or told to go back to their country (despite being U.S. citizens). Humans tend to form strong social bonds with individuals and groups who share similar characteristics and beliefs. Thus we tend to prioritize and protect those in our group often at the expense of those outside of it. Even young children demonstrate "in-group" bias or toward groups in which they are members (Patterson & Bigler, 2006). As a result, a focus solely on emotional empathy may not be useful in reducing polarization or bridging differences (Jilani, 2020). This is why reading books that offer diverse perspectives, views, and lived experiences is important to help students develop empathy and compassion for people with different social identities and backgrounds.

What Does This Mean for Our Teaching?

It is easy to fall into the trap of returning to our favorite stories time and time again. They are familiar and beloved. Yet, much of the traditional canon of literature, even in elementary classrooms, tends to have been written by and about white people. As we consider texts for class read-alouds, shared reading, guided reading, book clubs, and our classroom libraries, we should intentionally select texts that provide access to multiple characters, experiences, and perspectives that go beyond the dominant narrative.

To introduce the work of perspective taking, many teachers begin with books such as *The True Story of Three Little Pigs* by Jon Scieszka. This story is told from the perspective of the wolf in the classic story of *The Three Pigs*. By positioning the wolf as the narrator telling his version of the story, the reader is positioned to consider additional context and an alternate perspective which disrupts the traditional narrative where the wolf is labeled as "big" and "bad". The humanization of the wolf in this story may result in greater empathy for the character who was traditionally vilified.

Beginning with familiar stories allows students to tap into their prior knowledge and use what they know about the characters, setting, and plot to consider how the story would shift when told from a different perspective. Books such as *The True Story of Three Little Pigs, Duck Rabbit* by Amy Krouse Rosenthal and Tom Litchenheld or *Hey, Little Ant* by Phillip and Hannah Hoose provide alternate perspectives which lend themselves to introductory perspective taking work and can help scaffold students for examining perspective across texts (Kelly et al., 2023a). By laying the foundation with these books, students will be better prepared for more serious discussions that involve perspective taking.

Another great example of using stories to teach perspectives happened one day in Katelyn's fourth-grade class. Kaelynn mentioned seeing the confederate flag when she was out shopping with her dad. When she asked him what it represented, he explained that it was a symbol of hate and racism. To express empathy for Kaelynn's concerns and to deepen her students' understanding of the history and different perspectives about the controversial symbol, Katelyn read the book, *That Flag* by Tameka Fryer Brown. In the story, two best friends attend a school field trip to the Southern Legacy Museum where Kiera notices "that flag" on display. After learning about its history and meaning, she becomes upset that this flag flies outside the home of her best friend Bianca, who is white.

After discussing the story, students wrote a letter to one of the characters (Kiera or Bianca). In her letter, McKenzie empathized with Kiera, sharing how she too was upset when she learned the confederate flag was a symbol of racism. She very maturely encouraged Kiera to talk to her friend Bianca to share her feelings with the hopes that Bianca would be empathetic and ask her parents to remove them.

> Dear Kiera,
> I understand the hurt you faced. It's okay to be upset. I was upset too when I learned the cruel actuality of the meaning of the fact. Why would someone put a flag up ... if you knew what it meant. So, I feel your pain. But I would share what you learn with Bianca. Maybe she would understand and ask her parents why they have it up, and maybe even ask them to take it down.

Karlee demonstrated her empathy for Bianca (the girl whose family displayed the flag) in her letter by acknowledging the importance of always learning and growing. Understanding that sometimes we don't know what we don't know, but that we have a responsibility to listen and grow, she wrote,

> Dear Bianca, it's not your fault you didn't know what the flag meant. You are still learning and don't ever blame yourself for something you didn't know.

Considering both characters' perspectives, Kaelynn chose to write to both girls in her letter (Figure 1.5). She acknowledged how difficult it must've been for Kiera to learn about the meaning of the confederate flag and why she was upset with Bianca. She also expressed empathy for Bianca and suggested that perhaps

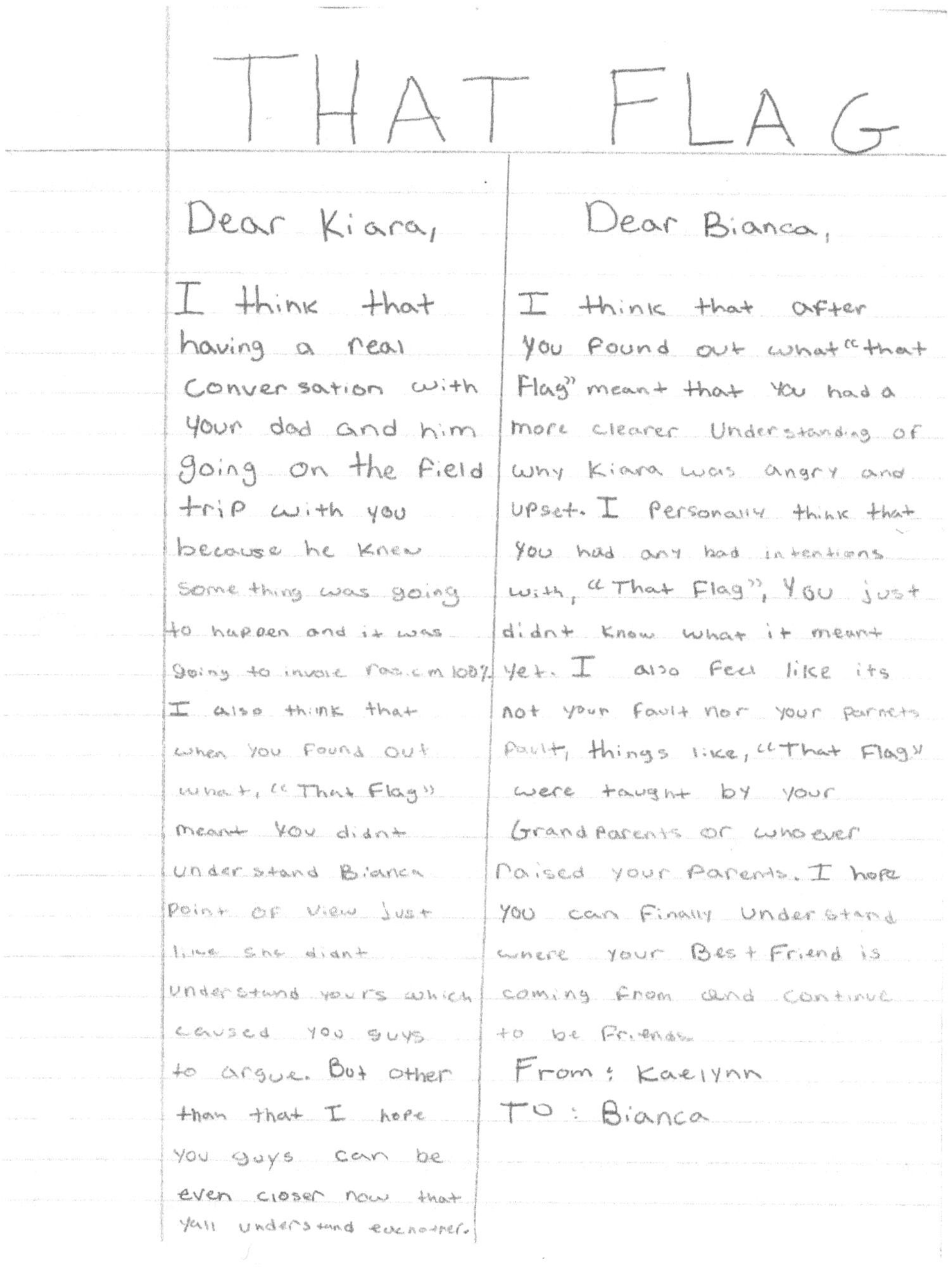

THAT FLAG

Dear Kiara,

I think that having a real conversation with your dad and him going on the field trip with you because he knew something was going to happen and it was going to invoke racism 100%. I also think that when you found out what, "That Flag" meant you didn't understand Bianca point of view just like she didn't understand yours which caused you guys to argue. But other than that I hope you guys can be even closer now that y'all understand eachother.

Dear Bianca,

I think that after you found out what "that Flag" meant that you had a more clearer understanding of why Kiara was angry and upset. I personally think that you had any bad intentions with, "That Flag", You just didn't know what it meant yet. I also feel like its not your fault nor your parents fault, things like, "That Flag" were taught by your Grandparents or whoever raised your parents. I hope you can finally understand where your Best Friend is coming from and continue to be Friends.

From: Kaelynn
To: Bianca

FIGURE 1.5

Kaelynn's Letter to the Characters in *That Flag*

she was unaware of the hateful symbolism of the flag due to the way the story of southern pride has been centered in her family over generations. Kaelynn explained, *"I am writing about both sides because I think that I understand Kiera the most but I kind of want to see Bianca's side because her parents had the flag up so I want to see if she knew what it meant already or not".*

Each of these examples reveals how reading can allow us to consider different perspectives without judgment. Beginning with literature allows us an opportunity to "try on" our empathy "attire" in settings where we are not intimately involved. It allows us to have a few "dress rehearsal" experiences as we build the language and attitudes before we are emotionally involved in a situation with a peer or family member. Through careful selection of texts, mature discussions with opportunities for empathetic listening and speaking in class, and application of perspective taking, students cultivate empathy and compassion.

Not Sure Where to Begin? Try This …

From Katie's first visit to Katelyn Barnett's fourth-grade classroom, she immediately knew that a strong classroom community had been established. Students sat where they felt most comfortable and many were open and vulnerable during mature class discussions. Katelyn uses children's literature as a springboard for these mature discussions to build community and cultivate compassion. In this section, we offer a description of her work and invite you to consider ways you and your students might engage in similar work.

Read-Alouds to Build Community, Engage in Mature Discussions, and Cultivate Compassion

Read-alouds offer many benefits including exposure to a variety of literature, concepts, and perspectives. They also create opportunities to build and sustain positive relationships and can serve as a springboard for mature and compassionate discussions in the classroom. Building trusting relationships where students can be vulnerable is essential to engage in mature discussions. We can build trusting classroom communities by being open and vulnerable ourselves. When we model our own stories, reactions, feelings, and lived experiences we open a door to allow students to get to know us as human beings beyond the teacher. By creating opportunities for students to share about themselves and by setting guidelines and expectations for active listening, asking nonjudgemental questions to deepen understanding, and responding in empathetic and compassionate ways students will feel comfortable to take risks as learners. When a new community is formed at the beginning of the school year or when it changes with the arrival of a new student, for instance, it's important to cultivate a trusting community. When we take the time to create community, students can thrive and be their authentic selves, be open-minded, take risks, and share a commitment towards collective action for the common good.

We can begin by reading books that celebrate students' identities, cultures, interests, and knowledge (Table 1.1). Create opportunities for students to share about themselves by connecting with various characters, settings, and situations in literature and with one another. This not only fosters a sense of belonging but

TABLE 1.1
Books to Celebrate Identity

Title	Focus
Alma and How She Got Her Name by Juana Martinez-Neal	Celebration of identity through names, family heritage, and culture.
The Day You Begin by Jacqueline Woodson	Celebrate who you are, even when you feel different.
A Different Pond by Bao Phi	A young Vietnamese American boy learns more about his culture when joins his father on early morning fishing trips to provide food for their family.
Dreamers by Yuyi Morales	Mexican-American author's immigration story.
Fry Bread by Kevin Noble Maillard	Celebration of identity through traditional Native American food.
I Am Enough by Grace Byers	Celebration of identity through empowering messages focused on self-worth and positive self-image.
I Am Every Good Thing by Derrick Barnes	Celebration of identity through affirmations and self-empowerment.
Love My Hair by Natasha Anastasia Tarpley	A young Black girl celebrates her identity through the love and appreciation of her natural hair.

TABLE 1.1 (Continued)

Title	Focus
Just Ask! by Sonia Sotomayor	Celebration of how different abilities, conditions, and challenges such as ADHD, diabetes, and hearing impairments can be strengths.
Looking Like Me by Walter Dean Myers	A young boy examines his various individual traits (appearance, family background, interests, etc.) and comes to appreciate who he is.
The Proudest Blue by Ibtihaj Muhammad with S.K. Ali	Young Faizah admires her older sister's hijab and demonstrates pride in her faith and cultural identity.
Skin Again by bell hooks	Celebration of identity through affirmation and beauty of skin color.
Sparkle Boy by Lesléa Newman	Celebration of self-expression by presenting a boy who is free to express himself (including choice of clothing) in a way that feels authentic to him.
Sulwe by Lupita Nyong'o	This book addresses colorism as a young girl with the help of her mother helps her come to accept her dark skin as beautiful and special.

also helps students make connections with those around them. Students begin to discover similarities among their classmates as well as things that make each individual unique. For example, Katelyn read *I Am Every Good Thing* by Derrick Barnes to celebrate Black joy and genius and to celebrate students' identities through the creation of "I Am" poems using a similar structure to that in the book (Figure 1.8). During a second read of the book, Katelyn encouraged students to read as writers to notice the author's craft moves. Specifically, she asked them to notice the kinds of things he wrote about using the stem "I Am …". As students shared examples from the book, Katelyn recorded them on a chart for future reference when writing their own "I Am" poems (Figure 1.6).

FIGURE 1.6

Students Brainstorm "I Am" Poems

In their poems, students shared their fears such as being in crowded spaces and getting lost. Some students shared their preference for listening to calming sounds like ocean waves, favorite foods (crab legs were popular), smells (vanilla, caramel, and fresh laundry), annoying siblings, and the upcoming basketball season. By sharing their poems with the class, students learned more about their peers and found commonalities. When reading their poems to the class, the room erupted in "me toos!" along with the quiet hand signal indicating agreement.

Teachers also learn more about their students through their responses to intentionally selected read-alouds that celebrate identity. As we get to know the students in our care, we learn valuable information to help us tailor instruction, select additional read-alouds, and facilitate compassionate discussions responsive to students' academic, social, and emotional needs.

Sometimes these needs are responsive to situations that occur throughout the school day. For instance, after a conflict occurred on the playground that resulted in a physical altercation, fourth-grade teacher Madison Siekman gathered her students on the carpet and invited them to share their thoughts and feelings about the incident using a talking piece and "I statements". This helps to center the child's experiences and feelings without blame. One student requested the talking piece and remarked, "I wanted to punch him but I knew I'd get in trouble". Madison praised the student for using restraint and for being honest about their feelings. She asked him to explain what occurred from his perspective that resulted in him feeling angry and wanting to punch someone. She reminded the class that it was his turn to talk since he had the talking piece, but they would have an opportunity to share their perspective and feelings. After everyone had an opportunity to share, Madison read the book, *Be Strong* by Pat Zietlow Miller. to help students process their feelings using nonviolent conflict resolution. After reading, students brainstormed ways they could demonstrate their strength beyond physical strength. They responded that they could be strong by walking away, listening, speaking up, and being brave (Kelly et al., 2023b). Listening to their peers' "I statements" provides students with opportunities to practice cognitive empathy ("The reason you feel this way is because …") and compassionate empathy ("We can do these things differently moving forward …"). This type of restorative approach focusing on problem-solving demonstrates the teacher's compassionate response rather than being punitive. Research shows that these types of restorative practices where students have opportunities to process together and discuss harm experienced or caused provide opportunities for problem-solving and reduced school discipline referrals.

The book *Be Strong* can also be used to help students embrace their emotions rather than suppress them. As fourth-grade teacher Katelyn explained, despite society sending us messages that crying is a sign of weakness, "it's ok to cry. If you cry, you're stronger. You care … You're empathetic". After reading *Be Strong*, Katelyn's class brainstormed what being strong is and isn't and recorded their responses on a chart (see Figure 1.7). One group noted that it is strong to stand up when someone is being bullied and to also stand up for the bully. Heer commented that a character in a book she recently read was kicking things because his dad died in a car accident. She continued to beautifully explain that while it may at first seem like his behavior is bad or unkind, it is important to better understand where people are coming from to understand their behavior without judgment. These fourth graders demonstrated compassion by considering a person's full humanity rather than forming an opinion based on

FIGURE 1.7

Students Create "strong" T Charts

FIGURE 1.8

Class Strengths Chain

one dimension or aspect (e.g. as a bully). As human beings, we are complicated and complex and thus we need to go beyond the surface level and get to know people better. This was a powerful lesson that served as a great springboard for the next lesson to continue building classroom community.

As an extension to the book *Be Strong*, Katelyn assigned each student a secret classmate to observe over the coming days. Specifically, she tasked them with observing the ways their classmates demonstrated strength. The following week students recorded their peers' strengths on a strip of paper and added them to a chain to symbolize the connection and collective strength of the class community (Figure 1.8).

When the chain was complete Katelyn explained, "The chain will remain hung up in our classroom. When you are feeling upset about something, when you are feeling down, when you're doing something or learning something that you don't feel confident in, when someone does or says something that makes you feel small, or less than … I want you to look up at this chain and I want you to remind yourself of all of the strengths in this classroom".

Voices from the Classroom

Katelyn Barnett, fourth grade teacher

"In a world where so much is out of our control, we, as teachers, have the unique privilege to develop beautiful people of empathy, understanding, and empowerment who can go out into that same world and be ripples of change. It is our responsibility as educators to not only disrupt the pre-packaged, limited perspective curriculum, but to also equip our students with the desire and confidence to advocate for themselves within and beyond our classroom walls".

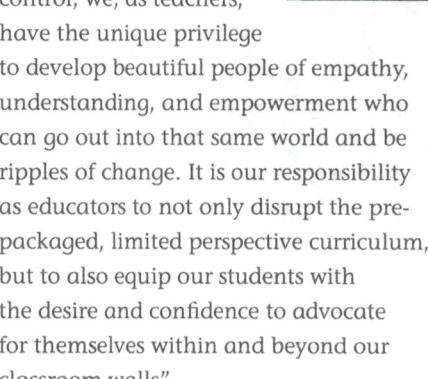

As described in the previous examples, carefully selected read-alouds can serve as foundational bedrocks for celebrating individual and collective identities, building classroom community, and supporting students socially and emotionally. Read-alouds can also empower and inspire students as change makers.

Classroom Example

From Reading About Change Makers Toward Taking Action: "Why Not?" Writing as a Tool for Change

Katelyn built on earlier read-alouds and compassionate discussions to help prepare students for action projects. She revisited the book *Be Strong* and encouraged students to consider the ways many individuals demonstrate strength when taking a stand for something they care about. She asked students to consider strong people in their lives and throughout history. Katelyn displayed photographs of change makers like Greta Thunberg and Malala Yousefzai. She displayed Norman Rockwell's "The Problem We All Live With" painting of six-year-old Ruby Bridges. Students discussed how Ruby Bridges was strong and brave being all alone (except for the U.S. Marshals who escorted her) walking by racist people spewing hateful comments as she entered her new school.

She also shared a photograph of Mister Rogers cooling his feet with Officer Clemmons in a small plastic pool to help students understand that segregation affected many aspects of people's lives beyond school. She explained that Mister Rogers and Officer Clemmons were strong to take action in response to the injustice of segregated public swimming pools.

KATELYN: We had segregated pools all over the country. Right down the street as well … Chloe, your grandma taught me this and showed me where it was. There was a pool where only Black people could go. Mister Rogers went on national television for everyone to see and invited his friend, this policeman, to put his feet in the water with him, knowing that some people, people with ugly hearts, would go, oh my gosh, why are they doing this? But Mister Rogers did it on purpose. Why?

MYKIE: Because he wanted to show … that they're all the same.

SARIYAH: There's nothing wrong with sharing a pool.

MADISON: He's trying to show that Black people aren't bad.

In addition to the books listed in Table 1.2, Katelyn read books such as *Gordon Parks: How the Photographer Captured Black and White America* by

TABLE 1.2
Books to Build Community

Title	Focus/Activities
Be Strong by Pat Zietlow Miller	Explore different ways to show strength (beyond physical strength) and resilience in difficult situations.
Brave Every Day by Trudy Ludwig	Discuss what it means to be brave and how to demonstrate empathy in the classroom. Have students act out scenarios from the book using role-play to practice problem-solving in a safe space.
Change Sings by Amanda Gorman	This book inspires a sense of collective responsibility. Encourage students to share stories when they made a difference and brainstorm ways to use their voices for change.
Circles All Around Us by Brad Montague	Circle students up as part of the morning meeting to share thoughts, feelings, experiences, and/or compliments. Discuss times when students felt included or excluded. Brainstorm ways to create circles of kindness in the classroom, school, and community.
Do Unto Otters: A Book About Manners by Laurie Keller	Discuss why it is important to treat people with respect and kindness. Encourage students to share a time when they felt respected or disrespected and how to apply these lessons to their interactions with classmates.
Each Kindness by Jacqueline Woodson	Discuss the missed opportunities to demonstrate kindness in the book. Ask "What could have been done differently?" Discuss the different perspectives included in the story and how the consideration of Maya's perspective can lead to empathy. Reflect on related experiences in their own lives.

TABLE 1.2 (Continued)

Title	Focus/Activities
Hello Neighbor!: The Kind and Caring World of Mister Rogers by Matthew Cordell	Discuss the ways Mister Roger teaches us about being a good neighbor. Encourage students to share times they demonstrated being a good neighbor and brainstorm ways to be kind to our classmates and broader community.
Malala's Magic Pencil by Malala Yousafzai	Share stories about a time when someone inspired them to make a difference. Encourage students to consider ways they can use their talents and efforts to improve their classroom and community.
Nobody Hugs a Cactus by Carter Goodrich	Discuss why the cactus felt lonely and how he changed when he connected with the bird. Invite students to share times when they have felt lonely. Brainstorm ways to build connections and how to help classmates who may feel lonely or left out.
Something, Someday by Amanda Gorman	Ask students to share about their hopes and dreams. Encourage them to consider ways to support one another in reaching our individual and collective goals.

Carole Boston Weatherford and *Until Someone Listens* by Estela Juarez to help students consider ways art, writing, and speaking can be tools for change. She then explained that they too can take a stand for something they care about. She introduced the "Why Not?" writing project by showing students a video of eleven-year-old Meghan Markle who wrote a letter to the company about their sexist dish soap advertisement (Figure 1.9). Next, she invited them to begin brainstorming issues that concerned them. Students shared concerns about equity in their school, equitable representation in the curriculum, protecting wildlife, and safety in their neighborhood.

FIGURE 1.9

Students View Video of Meghan Markle

"Why Not?" Projects

1. Introduce the why not project with an example of young people taking action for a cause they care about (e.g. video of Megan Markle writing letter to dish soap company).

2. Share about some issues you care about as other examples. Name them and provide an explanation about why you are concerned.

3. Invite students to brainstorm a list of issues and why they matter in their notebooks.

4. Provide time for students to share and create a class anchor chart.

5. Return to a familiar example. Review the issue and why it matters (e.g. dish soap ad only shows women washing the dishes which may reinforce gender stereotypes). Then frame it by asking "Why Not?" – why not do something about it? What can be done? (e.g. Megan Markle wrote a letter to the company describing her concerns and asking them to change the commercial to be more inclusive).

6. Ask students to brainstorm what kinds of actions they could take to address their issues of concern. Provide support as needed. Some students may want to brainstorm in their notebooks, other students may want to process orally with a partner or small group, and in some cases, it may be beneficial to discuss ideas as a whole group.

FIGURE 1.10
Completing Speed Bump
Request Form

One student completed an application to have speed bumps installed in her neighborhood to increase safety by encouraging drivers to slow down (see Figure 1.10). She also contacted her apartment complex so they too could submit the request forms.

Some students wrote letters to the district head nurse as well as the Johnson & Johnson Company regarding the lack of affordable access to brown skin-toned Band-Aids.

Karlee's Letter to the School District Head Nurse

Dear Ms. XXX and XXX School District,

Hello! My name is Karlee, and I am a fourth grade student at XXX School. I am writing to you today about band aids. [The district] only provides one type and color of band aids to students. I do not think it is very fair because students are all different colors and shades. When I need a band aid and am given a light colored band aid, it makes me feel different from others. The band aid does not match my skin and makes me think I am very, very different from other students. Dominique Apollon shared in his interview with NBC News in April of 2019, "It has taken me 45 trips around the sun but for the first time I know what it feels like to have a bandaid in my own skin tone". It shouldn't have taken 45 years for him to see a band aid his skin tone. I don't know why the school district thinks it is okay to have one color band aid. I hope you can fix this problem and give us darker colored band-aids for darker students.

Sincerely,

your friend Karlee

When Karlee received a response from the school district's head nurse regarding her inquiry about Band-Aids a few weeks later, she was overjoyed (see Figure 1.11).

KARLEE: *I got a response from writing about my Band-Aids and how there's not enough color Band-Aids at the school and the district nurse replied! A few weeks after that, the [school nurse] emailed Ms. Barnett and told her she has different varieties of Band-Aids now. And I saw one because I had to go in there and get a Band-Aid, and she has a bunch of different skin tones and a bunch of fun color ones!*

Karlee returned to class with her tie-dyed Band-Aid smiling ear to ear after visiting the school nurse exclaiming, "Look what I got!". When reflecting on the results of her Why Not? writing project Karlee shared, "It made me feel like I don't have to feel like not belonging when I have to have a Band-Aid like my skin color ... I don't have to feel like an outsider".

May 2, 2024

Dear Karlee,

Thank you for your letter outlining your concerns about the band aids _____ School District provides. I shared your experience of how a light-colored band aid makes you feel different from other students with the district's department responsible for ordering supplies. I recommended they consider purchasing band aids to match different skin tones and they assured me they would look into my request. I appreciate you sharing your viewpoint and hope we can bring about change together.

Best Regards,

FIGURE 1.11

District Nurse Response About Band-Aids

This is a powerful example that demonstrates the importance of inclusion and the ways young people can take action to make a difference in their lives and the lives of those around them. The district head of nursing demonstrated compassion for Karlee as she considered the ways that she may have felt othered by only having access to Band-Aids for lighter skin. Writing for change is empowering and shows students how their voices can bring a concern or issue to the surface and result in a satisfactory change. It also demonstrates the significance of asking and seeking information to further understand rather than assuming a lack of interest. Since we don't know what we don't know, we often do not recognize a problem until someone brings it to our attention.

Kaelynn received the following letter from Johnson & Johnson in response to her letter about the need for more affordable skin tone Band-Aids (Figures 1.12 and 1.13).

Another powerful example of the ways students used writing to demonstrate compassion for those who have been othered or silenced came about during

Voices from the Classroom

Karlee, fourth grader

"The power of me writing the letter to the district about a problem our whole community has had is really special to me because I think everybody in the whole school who looks like me had a problem with it but they never thought to write anything to them … People were worried they'd get in trouble … I just thought if I tried to say something then maybe something would change. And that is the impact of the beautiful Band-Aids we have now".

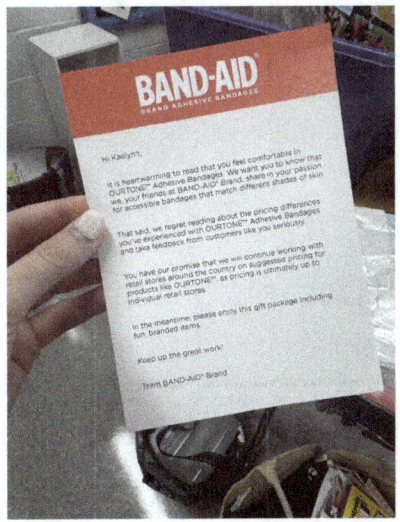

FIGURE 1.12
Letter from Johnson & Johnson

FIGURE 1.13

Kaelynn Proudly Displays Skin Tone Band-Aids

their study about westward expansion. Katelyn's students unanimously agreed that the textbook, Savvas' My World Interactive, represented mostly the white settlers' perspective and offered very limited information about the Indigenous people who were on the land long before the settlers arrived and claimed it as their own. With the students gathered on the carpet, Katelyn concluded a lesson examining the perspectives included and thus excluded and closed the textbook. As she prepared to move on from the lesson, Kaelynn chimed in, "Wait, why are all the kids on the cover of the textbook white? It catches me off guard". This comment later became the springboard for an inquiry and "Why Not?" writing project to the textbook company.

After much discussion and exploration of the textbook, two students chose to write letters to the publisher expressing their concerns about the lack of representation of diverse people on the cover of their social studies book.

Lily's Letter to Publisher

February 28, 2024

Dear Publisher,

My name is Lily. I'm upset that your textbook cover only has one type of skin tone which is white. I am Mexican and seeing this makes me feel like I'm not important. Natasha Capers once said in her article 'Why It's Critical for Students to "See Themselves" in Classroom Materials' that "when children aren't seeing themselves represented it sends them a message". Since your cover doesn't represent any skin tone but the color white, the message it tells everyone who isn't white is *"you're not important!"* When you make a cover with only white students you're agreeing with the people who think you only teach one side of history. Your cover makes me and other people feel like you're only going to teach the white Americans' side of history.

Since your textbook is called MyWorld you can let the world see that all skin tones should be seen as equal. Natasha Capers also writes in the same article that "studies have proven that reading is an important tool for improving emotional intelligence and empathy in children". Your textbook doesn't have this because the cover is teaching kids that the white side of history is more important than the native. All my classmates (who are black, Indian, mixed) agree with me, and they say they are upset about the cover. I know my teacher isn't comfortable teaching history when the history textbook has all white students when her class has no white students. Teaching kids about skin tones, how some look, shouldn't be overlooked, but your textbook does overlook this just on the cover.

I hope you have a change of heart and change your textbook cover.

Sincerely,

Lily

To their surprise, Savvas contacted Katelyn and requested to visit the class. They were impressed with the students' letters and said they'd never received this kind of input from students. This unprecedented action inspired them to schedule a visit to their classroom to listen to students' concerns. The students were shocked! Kaelynn's jaw dropped when she heard the news. Lily exclaimed, "*Writing can be so powerful! I didn't know I could do that!*"

During their visit, the students shared their concerns with the Savvas's representatives and listened respectfully to their responses. The representatives explained that they appreciated the students' insight and that they want to do better moving forward. Lily reflected on how validating and empowering the experience was.

Voices from the Classroom

Lily, fourth grader

"[The textbook publishers] all took turns actually saying how they felt and what they felt when we sent them letters. One of them even said, oh my, holy moly, this is amazing. And it filled my heart, made my heart feel so happy".

They acknowledged the students' concern about the cover and explained that because the design zoomed in on the state of South Carolina on the map, the student of color (as seen on the cover on the website) was cropped out. They explained that they have taken the students' concerns into consideration and the company plans to update the cover in the next few years as a result.

The students also expressed concerns about the lack of diverse authors. They explained that more diverse contributors the textbook would create greater inclusivity and broader perspectives when creating content for young readers. Although the company noted that there are in fact authors of color, they agreed that it was problematic that their names and photos weren't included in the acknowledgments and plan to update the author page accordingly.

As critically civic-minded young people, Katelyn's students remained hopeful but continued with further inquiries. For example, McKenzie was dismayed with the publisher's response that they limit the amount of "extraneous" content because the state will cut content not aligned with state standards. Referring to historically marginalized perspectives as "extraneous" in and of itself is problematic and demonstrates the need for further inclusion of diverse voices. McKenzie suggested they write to the state to change the standards to be more inclusive of historically marginalized perspectives.

Empathy and compassion are the foundation of a democratic society (Mirra, 2018). Students in Sarah's and Katelyn's fourth-grade classrooms have learned valuable lessons in empathy and compassion as change agents. Through the exploration of perspective taking, learning honest history, and considering the role of power, these young people are positioned to think critically and compassionately and use their voices as a tool of activism to make a change. They learned to conduct research to examine credibility and explore multiple sources including different perspectives to be more informed. They used reading, writing, listening, and speaking skills to deepen their understanding and communicate with their peers and adults within and beyond the school building to cultivate empathy and compassion for change in their lives and the lives of people in their community. As Mirra notes, "If we are able to adopt the perspectives of those unlike ourselves, then perhaps we are more likely to make decisions and take steps that benefit not only our own selfish interests, but the interests of those other people as well" (2018, p. 4).

Yet, schools often reduce the teaching of empathy to a focus on kindness and following the "golden rule" (treat people the way you want to be treated) rather than true perspective taking (Mirra, 2018). Teaching soft skills and good citizenship are common practices in schools and many social emotional learning (SEL) curricula. Instead, we can help students develop empathy and compassion that goes beyond surface-level notions of kindness and individuality that risk maintenance of an inequitable status quo (Mirra, 2018). This approach limits one's ability to consider and take into account the larger contextual factors and social constructs that influence our individual and collective lives. In the next chapter, we will explore ways to engage students in developing an understanding of current issues in the news.

> **PAUSE AND REFLECT**
>
> Reflect on how your understanding of empathy and compassion has shifted after reading this chapter. In what ways can you help students develop as empathetic and compassionate citizens within and beyond your classroom?

> Literature provides a safe space to practice empathy. Yet access to books (particularly those featuring people from historically marginalized groups) has increasingly been limited across the U.S. In response to this ongoing censorship, fourth graders in D.C. protested book bans and wrote a letter to Scholastic in response to their 2023 "opt-out" offering of "diverse books". To read the letter and learn more: https://www.dcareaeducators4socialjustice.org/news/4th-graders-challenge-book-bans-and-scholastic

CHAPTER 2
Helping Students Become More Aware of Issues Within the Community

TEACHER: Who else has a news article today? Maya?

MAYA: So last week was the end of Passover and I'm Jewish, if you didn't know that. So last week this nineteen-year-old boy came into the synagogue and he was a gunman and he shot two people. And the Rabbi, he was trying to protect everyone who was in the synagogue. This woman was trying to protect the Rabbi and then they both got shot.

TEACHER: Maya, I thought about sharing that news story yesterday but I decided not to because any time there are stories that have violence like that I always want to think real carefully about "Do I share it?" And if I do share it, how will I share it? But I should have because people hear about it. You knew about it.

MAYA: Yeah, when I heard that I felt really mad because as you know Jewish people are very open. Jewish people say, like, "We're all family". Even if we don't know each other, we're all family.

TEACHER: But somehow this man had some really awful thoughts?

MAYA: Yeah, when he came in the synagogue he started saying bad things about Jewish people, and this man, he must have been really, really strong and not scared at all, because he chased that nineteen-year-old boy out of that synagogue. Caleb?

CALEB: Why would the nineteen-year-old gunman do it?

MAYA: Because he was someone who just liked white people, like white, Christian people.

There are plenty of rationalizations we draw upon when choosing to avoid the news in our classrooms. For one, we may assume our students won't understand, or maybe even care about, what's going on. There are also times when we worry about what our classroom parents or administrators might say. Additionally, as in the vignette shared from Chris' second-grade classroom above, we may worry that a particular issue will be too frightening for children. This is a dilemma we've all faced – to share or not to share. Yet, as Maya demonstrates through her honest reflections as a proud member of the Jewish community, our students are already impacted by these stories.

In the wake of 9/11 and the 2017 bombings in Brussels, Holly McGhee was contemplating this very issue – how do kids process the news they hear? This led her to write a picture book intended to help children feel less frightened of the world around them. The book, *Come With Me,* opens with a small girl sitting alone in front of a large TV screen. Her body is rigid and her face solemn as she stares into the nightly news. The text reads,

> All over the world, the news told
> and told
> and retold
> of anger and hatred –
>
> People against people.
>
> And the little girl was frightened
> by everything she heard
> and saw
> and felt.

Feeling unsettled, the girl goes to find her papa and asks what she can do to make the world a better place. Her papa takes her out into the neighborhood to help her understand that rather than living in fear, one thing she can do is actively connect with the people within her neighborhood. Later, her mama leads her to other parts of the neighborhood, helping her acknowledge and take strength from the wonderful diversity of people found there. In doing so, each of her parents helps her see that the news does not always fully, or fairly, represent the world outside her door. McGhee writes,

> [They] were brave and kind,
> and that day
> they won a tiny battle
> over fear
> for themselves
> and for the people of the world.

We think about this book often when advocating for brave spaces like Maya's second-grade classroom above – classrooms where young children have an open invitation to talk about what they've heard, discuss how it makes them feel, and seek to understand what it all means. Consider for a moment: What if instead of encouraging Maya to share, Chris had said, "School really isn't the place to talk about these things?" Being well versed in cowering behind classroom furniture during intruder drills, how might the children in that classroom have internalized news of a gunman entering a synagogue if no one was willing to help them process what had happened? Beyond this, how were they also internalizing other messages they received about racism, sexism, xenophobia, climate change, immigration, and other important issues within their local and broader communities?

Chris' initial reluctance to talk about the shooting in a synagogue ignored the fact that all of his students were affected by that news. They needed an outlet for their thoughts and worries to ensure these didn't become unchecked fears and anxieties that manifest themselves into behaviors and habits that are adverse to healthy social and emotional development. Remaining silent in response to important issues only serves to uphold the status quo and makes us complicit in sustaining systems of oppression and poor stewardship of the Earth. Willful silence is not a moral response to the needs of children; nor is it a moral response to the needs of a democracy.

Instead, we must institute classroom structures and instructional practices that invite children to not only share what they've already heard and noticed but also develop an awareness and growing understanding of other issues facing their communities as well. In this chapter, we show you how to support students in doing this very work.

Developing an Awareness and Understanding of Current Issues

It's not just that we sometimes avoid engaging with the news in our classrooms. There are times when we avoid these stories in our personal lives, as well. As much as we want to remain informed, studies have shown that as many as two-thirds of Americans feel worn out by the sheer amount of information being shared across online news outlets, television, radio, social media, phone notifications, and so on (Pew Research Center, 2020). Worse yet, when we spend significant amounts of time seeking out negative news (i.e. *doomscrolling*), we're more likely to suffer from anxiety, loss of sleep, and reduced life satisfaction (Arnand et al., 2022; Satici et al., 2023).

Our news consumption doesn't need to be this way. In fact, our classrooms can help children learn how to approach the news in a healthy way as students become well-informed on social, political, and environmental issues while celebrating positive stories and remaining ever hopeful for the world they're working to create for themselves and those around them. One way to achieve this is to help students think critically about the content found in the news. This is the work being done in *Come With Me*, as both parents help their daughter understand that their neighborhood and the people in it are far richer and more complex than what gets boiled down into a single news story.

We can do this too. For instance, we can facilitate an inquiry where our students keep a tally of how often the news reports negative stories versus positive ones and then discuss why stories of hope, goodwill, and accomplishment are less likely to be reported. Additionally, students can analyze new reports to determine what representation looks like in the new media – paying attention to how various groups of people are portrayed. After collecting their data, students can then invite a local journalist or news editor into the classroom to share their findings and ask critical questions such as:

> Why aren't there more positive stories in the news?
>
> How do you decide which stories get covered and which do not?
>
> Who tells the news? Who makes decisions about what news is shared?
>
> What determines where a story is placed in the newspaper or on a website?
>
> How do you approach media representation?
>
> How diverse is the staff making these decisions?
>
> How can we start sharing ideas for stories we think you should be covering?

This work is critical because, as the old adage states, *knowledge is power*. A well-informed citizenry who is willing and able to ask hard questions is better prepared to hold their elected officials – not to mention, the media – accountable for the important decisions they make. For instance, in her book *What the Fact?: Finding the Truth in All the Noise* (2022), Seema Yasmin reports a significant mismatch between who has the power to make key decisions about the news and the populations that are mostly likely to consume and be affected by these stories. She explains that people from minoritized racial and ethnic social groups made up nearly 40% of the U.S. population in 2021, yet less than one in five newsroom bosses came from these same populations. This is concerning because the viewpoints of white newsroom directors, regarding what is newsworthy, are often shaped by their own cultural and racial lenses and biases. This leads to important stories being overlooked or minimized. One example of this is the fact it took almost a year for national news outlets to finally cover the Flint Water Crisis, long ignoring a tragedy that disproportionately affected the Black community.

Furthermore, helping our students become well-informed helps to ensure they are connected to the world around them as they take joy in the success of various communities of people, as well as better understand and empathize with their struggles. Doing so provides opportunities for students to: (1) learn how to actively seek out important information about their communities, (2) learn about differing perspectives, and (3) begin to recognize opportunities to take meaningful action. Let's take a look at how we can accomplish each of these.

Actively Seeking Out the News

A long-accepted belief about responsible citizenship states that citizens must be well-informed on key issues in order to maintain a successful democracy. In years past, this took the form of morning newspapers and the nightly news. The past two decades have seen this news landscape change drastically. A study conducted by the Pew Research Center (2020) found that the majority of Americans now get their news from digital devices such as phones, tablets, and laptops and only a third reported their news often comes from dedicated news sites, with social media playing an increasingly large role in what stories are shared and how they are communicated. In research studying how news is consumed around the world, Gil de Zuniga et al. (2020) warned that with so many news items popping up in social media feeds, people are far more likely to feel as though they don't need to actively seek out the news. This new phenomenon, termed "The news finds me", is problematic in that people run the risk of becoming passive receivers of news and being more susceptible to misinformation as Facebook, Instagram, YouTube, TikTok, X, and other outlets become major players in determining what news is relevant and how it is shaped for consumers; thus, increasing the potential for ingroup bias from news sources that share the same perspectives as their readers.

What Does This Mean for Our Teaching?

We can begin by making sure our students are taught the importance of understanding what is going on in their communities. Note that we used the word *understand*, rather than know. This should not take the form of a traditional book report where students read a story and then offer up the highlights. Rather, responsibly consuming the news calls on each of us to carefully consider what we read, think about what it means to us in light of other things we've come to know, acknowledge how this makes us feel and why, and identify any lingering tensions or questions we want to research further. Our second task is to help children learn how to actively seek out news stories, rather than passively waiting to have the news come to them.

For example, second-grade teacher Tim O'Keefe, committed to teaching his students the importance of news literacy, places the local newspaper on a stool at the front of the classroom each morning. After a period of exploration time where children can come into the classroom and self-select what they would like to be working on, he brings them to a circle in the front of the room for what he refers to as *News and Journals*. This is a time each day when the kids talk about things going on in the news as well as other things they've been thinking about that they want their classmates to help them better understand.

For the first few months of the year, Tim does most of the sharing. He opens the newspaper and helps his young students understand what is going on in their city, nation, and world and then invites them to share their thoughts with prompts such as *What do you think about this?* or What *questions do you have?* In doing so, Tim models what it looks like to stay informed and to invite others to help him make sense of what he's read. Over the course of his two years with his students, he slowly hands over the reins to the children as they take on part of the responsibility for finding, sharing, and discussing important stories. Some of these come from their homes. Others come directly from the newspaper and online resources (such as the widely used Newsela site) that the kids access from their classroom laptops.

Learning About Differing Perspectives

Being informed also helps us learn about the presence of multiple perspectives. This calls on us to step outside of our (oft like-minded) social circles. This can be a real challenge because as political divisiveness continues to escalate, we are a nation becoming increasingly polarized. Studies show that our beliefs regarding key issues, from racial justice to immigration, play a significant role in determining who we talk to throughout the day and even where we choose to live (Brown & Enos, 2021). There are two significant issues with this. First, this polarization grows from the belief that people across the political spectrum agree on very little, if anything at all. Of course, this is not true. While there *are* stark differences that demand our attention, there is also some common ground. Yet, when polarization occurs, opportunities to use shared beliefs as a path forward are lost.

Secondly, when we insulate ourselves inside a homogenous bubble of like-minded folks, we lose out on opportunities to have our thinking challenged by those whose perspectives and lived experiences differ from our own; increasing the likelihood that we come to believe our community's shared thoughts and values are universal. When well-developed norms are established to ensure a productive and respectful exchange of ideas (see Chapter 3), such discussions can help people better understand one another as well as think more critically about their own beliefs and practices.

What Does This Mean for Our Teaching?

Being informed calls on us to be knowledgeable of multiple perspectives, especially when we don't necessarily agree with them. By teaching our students to have a respectful and productive dialogue, we provide a space where they can share openly and come to expect many of their peers to help them think more critically about important issues in the community. However, as demonstrated in this vignette, this is not to say that all perspectives shared will be accurate. The morning after the January 6, 2020 attack on the U.S. Capitol, Tianna Myers brought her fourth-grade class together for Morning Meeting. Teaching and learning in the midst of a global pandemic, her students logged into the virtual classroom from their homes and waited for the discussion to begin. While most classrooms across the country likely avoided the frightening events of January 6th, Tianna knew her kids would want to process this news together. Not far into the discussion, someone referred to what happened at the Capitol as a *riot*. Quickly, another student came off mute to clarify,

JAMIE: Actually, it wasn't a riot. They were protesting.

By the looks of her students' faces on the screen, Tianna could see that many disagreed. They had seen the footage of people scaling walls, busting down doors, breaking windows, destroying furniture, and ransacking offices. After a short pause, someone spoke up to challenge Jamie.

STACY: But they were breaking things. They were hurting people. That's not a protest.

JAMIE: Yeah it was. They were exercising their right to speak, to protest.

SAQUAN: But that's not a protest. They broke into the building. There was police telling them not to.

JAMIE: Besides, if Biden would have lost they would have done the same thing. People would have been really mad.

SAQUAN: How do you know that, Jamie?

STACY: Also Jamie, when Black Lives Matter has a protest there are police all over the place. They would have gone to jail.

KAYLA: That's right. My parents said that if those were Black people at the Capitol doing all that they would have been shot.

JAMIE: I don't know.

Voices from the Classroom

Tianna Myers

"There are a variety of sensitive topics that are discussed in morning meaning in my class – most of them being related to issues of race, ethnicity, gender identity, and sexual orientation. When these aren't talked about at home or haven't been discussed in past classrooms, they do feel some discomfort at first. But when they've lived these things, they're super passionate about talking about them. For example, my Black students are often very comfortable talking about race because even though they're in fourth and fifth grade, they've experienced the feeling of being othered or walking into a room and not having many people who look like them or that share cultural connections with them. Because families can be concerned about these sorts of discussions, I am very proactive. I explain what our morning meeting structure is for – inviting kids to bring in articles and questions about the world that they want us to discuss. I'm open and honest with families. I also invite them into the classroom because I want them to understand that I am not trying to force certain beliefs onto their children or put their children into a place of discomfort based on who they are".

– Tianna Myers, fourth and fifth-grade teacher

PAUSE AND REFLECT

Pause for a moment and create a list of all the things you are already providing your students that support them to develop the skills and agency necessary for taking action. Next, create a list of what you believe they may still need that could become part of your future teaching.

In this short exchange, everyone had an opportunity to hear how people in class were thinking and feeling about what had happened. In the process, students continued to learn that an important part of critical dialogue is to challenge one another in ways that attempt to speak truth to the topic but also, void of rancor and name-calling, encourage those around them to be willing to listen.

Recognizing Opportunities for Action

When we are well-informed, we are much more likely to be civically engaged. For instance, a study by the Center for Information and Research on Civic Learning and Engagement (2023) found that while 76% of young voters felt their age group has the power to create change, more than half said they lacked the information and support they needed to be politically active. This was most evident with students of Color, of which only a third felt they possessed the information and support they required. This resulted in few young people participating in political activities such as signing petitions or attending protests and demonstrations – despite many reporting that they would be interested in doing so in the future. This begs us to ask, with such opportunities *already* available to them, what should we be doing in our classrooms to set our youngest citizens on a trajectory toward action?

What Does This Mean for Our Teaching?

More than simply teaching students to acquire information and skills as part of their schooling, we must help them recognize that new information has the capacity to change them in important ways. In doing so, there are times when it feels appropriate to end our discussions or units of study with the simple-yet-powerful question *Now what?*, nudging students toward action. When we build conversations about what we can or should do with what we've learned, we help students see a connection between the learning that takes place in our classrooms and opportunities to live in a different sort of way – becoming more informed, more agentive, and more just.

For example, to frame the literacy work they would be doing together in their second-grade classroom, Chris asked his students, *Why is it important that we grow into stronger readers, writers, listeners, and speakers?* As one might expect, initial responses spoke to strong report cards, preparedness for state testing, being able to read more complex books, feeling prepared for third grade, and eventually getting into a good college. Not satisfied, Chris pointed out there are many other reasons we need to develop strong literacy skills. After a few moments, one of the quietest children in the classroom raised her hand and responded, "So we can stand up for ourselves".

Her classmates looked confused. They weren't sure what to make of this. They knew it sounded like it should be right but they struggled to give examples of what this might look like in practice. With some prompting, they soon started talking about a book that showed how Malala Yousafzai used her literacy skills to secure greater education rights for children across the globe. Other stories emerged too: the research they had conducted before lobbying a state senator, the fifth-grade class who had once studied the underrepresentation of women on city landmarks and made speeches at City Hall, the times they had used their words to talk out problems before they could escalate into a fight, and having read news articles about unfair dress codes to better understand the expectations the school district placed upon different social groups within their own local schools. Over the remainder of the year, when the class learned about a problem that felt important to them, they were prepared to stop and consider, *How can we use our reading, writing, listening, and speaking skills to learn more about this and to maybe even try to make it better?* This is an essential step in our teaching, helping our students see that learning in the classroom prepares them for a civic life where they strive to make positive change.

> ## Picture Books Showing Literacy as a Tool for Action
>
> The following picture books tell the story of agentive citizens using literacy as a tool for social and political action. These books provide students with a vision for what they're own collaborative and individual work can look like.
>
> *Ida B. Wells, Voice of Truth* (2022) by Michelle Duster
>
> *The Power of Her Pen, The Story of Groundbreaking Journalist Ethel L Payne* (2020) by Lisa Cline-Ransome
>
> *Carter Reads the Newspaper* (2019) by Margaret Hopkinson
>
> *I Dissent: Ruth Bader Ginsberg Makes Her Mark* (2016) by Debbie Levy
>
> *What Do You Do with a Voice Like That?: The Story of Extraordinary Congresswoman Barbara Jordan* (2018) by Chris Barton

Not Sure Where to Begin? Try This…

One of many obstacles that keeps us from incorporating current news into our classrooms is a feeling that there just isn't enough time in the day to do "one more thing". This concern is understandable because there really is so much to do. That said, when we carefully integrate current news into the work we're already doing alongside our students, building greater awareness of the issues in their communities, nation, and world becomes a seamless part of our classroom structures and curriculum. In this section, we will detail how you can provide your students opportunities to share their observations, questions, and concerns, as well as how you can integrate news articles and issue-based children's literature into your curriculum.

Providing Students Opportunities to Share Their Observations, Questions, and Concerns

The first step we can take in helping students become more aware is to build a predictable structure that invites them to share their observations and the questions and concerns that emerge from these. This act of observing and questioning calls on students to do critical work as they learn to take notice of those things around them that appear to lack adequate logic, explanation, or justice and then invite those around them into discussion to help them try to make sense of these things (Hass, 2020). For instance, a student might ask, *Why don't the boys ever pass the football to the girls at recess? What makes a bad word so bad?*, or *Why are most superheroes white?*

When we carefully scaffold our students into observing the world more closely, asking critical questions, and then engaging in discussion with their peers, we begin to live into Paulo Friere's (2000) vision of a liberatory education where students are not only learning to read the word, but to read the *world*. Reading the world means students take in information from all they see and hear and then engage in critical thought that leads to new learning, helping them to better understand their communities. This work positions students as agentive meaning-makers who engage in social critique as a means of creating a more just world. This work begins by implementing classroom journals into our daily morning meeting.

Launching Classroom Journals in the Morning Meeting

Classroom journals (Hass, 2020; Mills, O'Keefe, & Jennings, 2004) are a place where students record the observations and questions they'd like to share with their classmates during morning meeting. This could be a special notebook, a stack of large drawing paper that's been stapled together, or even a shared Google Doc. No matter what form your classroom journals take, the goal is to have a dedicated space where students can begin recording their observations and questions so they are prepared to share these with the class.

Of course, this work is going to look different at various grade levels. For instance, in Taylor Wuerfel's kindergarten class, she created a single Book of Wonders journal where her five- and six-year-old students could jot down some of the things they were curious about (see Figure 2.1). As you might imagine, this took a good bit of modeling on her part to help her students understand what this journal was for, the difference between a statement and a question, how they would go about crafting sentences that began with a capital letter and ended a with a question mark, and how they would use the Book of Wonders to invite their friends into discussion. To create space for this work, Taylor carved out about ten minutes from their morning meeting for student-led discussions stemming from their questions.

Always looking for opportunities to take action, Taylor leveraged one of her students' questions, *Why does so much food get thrown away at lunch?*,

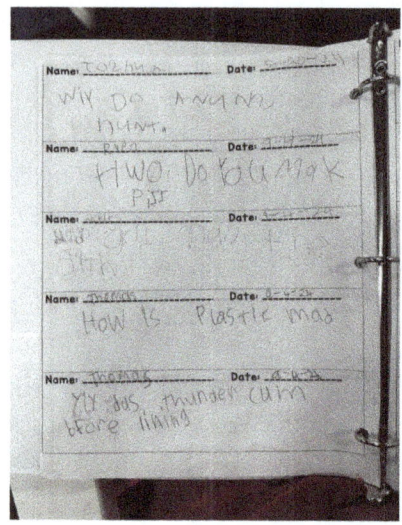

FIGURE 2.1

Student Entries in the Kindergarten Book of Wonders

Voices from the Classroom

Taylor Wuerfel

"Morning meetings center my student's voices and give us an opportunity to have rich discussions as a community. I find that most authentic learning comes from the questions students ask, as they lead to profound conversations and invite many perspectives. Most importantly, morning meetings give students a sense of autonomy and agency. The kids' questions lead to discussions, discussions lead to new learning, and that new learning helps us take action. My advice for teachers starting their own morning meeting journey is to follow your students. You'll be surprised, in the best way, at how much you'll learn with them".

– Taylor Wuerfel, kindergarten teacher

into an opportunity to learn more about composting and to begin a class project where they collected compostable waste to reduce the amount of garbage going into the landfill (see Figure 2.2).

Working with older students, Nozsa Kyler approaches this work a little differently. Her second and third-grade classroom offers a variety of different journals, including a Science Journal, Language Journal, Math Journal, Classroom Community Journal, and Culture Journal (see Figure 2.3). Having multiple journals helps her students begin thinking about how careful observation and questioning support their understanding across various disciplines.

FIGURE 2.2

Kindergartners Prepare to Collect Compostable Waste from the Cafeteria

Nozsa explains,

> In our classroom morning meeting, I set high expectations for my kids. They know this is a place where they need to be present both physically and mentally. They need to seek knowledge about what is happening in our community and to think critically about the problems those in the community face. And they need to make room to hear from a variety of people and to think up with them – even on issues and topics that don't directly affect them. Classroom journals help us do all this.

Of course, students will need to be supported in this work. At first, this will call on you to provide lots of scaffolding. Your students may need to spend a few weeks watching you record your own observations and questions and then inviting them into discussion before they are ready to tackle this work themselves. When you feel they are ready, you can support your students into

FIGURE 2.3

Classroom Journals in Nozsa Kyler's Classroom

success by generating questions alongside them in response to a book you're reading, being on the lookout for questions that emerge throughout the day as you listen in on their conversations, and even invite their families to help them think of questions that have come up at home (Hass, 2020). With time and support, they will begin to generate lots of great queries (see Table 2.1) that elicit rich discussion.

Integrating News Articles and Issue-based Books into the Classroom

In addition to creating a daily structure where students share current news and critical questions, it's also important to integrate news articles and issue-based books into the current curriculum. This is similar to the work many teachers already do when selecting culturally relevant texts to celebrate the social identities within their classrooms and schools. These teachers understand that we cannot blindly follow every aspect of the prescriptive curricula and resources that are pushed onto us by our districts and states. Rather, we teach literacy skills through carefully selected texts we know will build greater engagement (Jones & Lynch, 2023; Marquez & Colby, 2021) while

TABLE 2.1

Sample Student Questions from a Third-Grade Classroom

Classroom Community Journal
Why is it when I set up a game, no one wants to play with me?
Why do people in our class fight about the tiny things?
Why do people use mean language?
What language is allowed in our classroom?
Why do people say "cheater" so often?
Why are people going down the slide two at a time when we're not supposed to?
Why do people put their hands on each other?

Culture Journal
Why are there weapons to hurt people?
Why do we have all the wars?
Why does the middle finger mean bad things?
Why do some white people treat Black people badly?
What makes a book inappropriate?
Where does the first person in your family get their last name?
Why do we turn religious things into presents and candy?
Why do we have different countries?
Why doesn't our money have pictures of women on it?
Why were Nerf guns invented if they teach you bad things?
Should kids play violent video games?

also helping students better understand themselves and those around them (Bishop, 1990).

Selecting resources that grow student awareness follows this same premise, accessing texts that focus on issues such as belonging, justice, and equity when teaching reading and writing skills. Integrating these types of issue-based books and news articles beautifully compliments the culturally relevant books we're already using because while one affirms and celebrates various social identities (as defined by race, ethnicity, gender, religion, socio-economic status, personal interests, etc.), the other helps students see how these same attributes sometimes result in the oppressive treatment of entire communities of people. Combining these two types of texts – celebratory and critical – allows us to construct an important tool for our teaching, critical text sets.

Creating Critical Text Sets

For the purposes of this work, we're defining critical text sets as a collection of books that acknowledge and celebrate a particular social identity as well as introduce students to the struggles and injustices people within these communities sometimes experience. The first step in selecting which critical text sets to use is to determine what issues you want to explore alongside your students. For instance, perhaps someone in the class has shared a news story about a significant increase in the number of people coming across the southern U.S. border and you want to select texts about immigration that will humanize this issue. Being responsive to student interests, questions, and tensions is certainly important when determining where to begin. Conversely, perhaps there has been an issue in the news you want to share with your kids at Morning Meeting (say, the plight of both Jews and Palestinians) but it makes sense to first read a few books together to gain some needed context before having that discussion. Read-alouds do a wonderful job of providing students with shared knowledge they can draw upon when trying to make sense of complex issues.

Secondly, we have to consider how these texts will meet the specific needs of our literacy instruction. The developmental readiness of our students, as well as the content we are teaching (i.e. strategies for decoding, use of text features, cause and effect, etc.) will shape which texts best fit the demands of our curriculum. While the suggested books in Table 2.2 serve as a great place to begin selecting the books you might use, there are incredibly helpful resources online that can help you find exactly what you need. One piece of advice we have for the process of selection, however, is to make certain students have ample opportunities to engage with stories that provide affirmations of identity. We do not want to reduce the rich lives and accomplishments of any group of people to just those stories that focus on the injustices they face.

Lastly, while there are many high-quality picture books at the ready to help students build greater awareness about important issues, it's important that we also access news articles as a classroom resource for literacy instruction. News articles provide timely, real-world examples of how these issues play out in our communities. For instance, after reading books that acknowledge and affirm those with significantly limited income, a news article about the effect of rising food prices, efforts to make school lunches free for all students, or community programs to address food scarcity would offer students an opportunity to learn how low wages and unemployment affects those within their community.

TABLE 2.2

Critical Text Sets

Topic	Books That Affirm	Books That Demonstrate Struggle
Belonging	*All Are Welcome* by A. Penfold *We Are Grateful* by T. Sorell *The Day You Begin* by J. Woodson	*The Invisible Boy* by T. Ludwig
Difference	*Eyes That Kiss in the Corners* by J. Ho *You Are Enough* by M. O'Hair *I Like Myself!* By K. Beaumont	*Mixed* by A. Chung
Families	*A Family is a Family is a Family* by S. O'Leary *Stella Brings the Family* by M.B. Schiffer *Families, Families, Families!* By S. Lang	*The Case for Loving: The Fight for Interracial Marriage* by S. Alko
Gendered Expectations for Boys	*Julian is a Mermaid* by J. Love *My Princess Boy* by C. Kilodavis *Pink is For Boys* by R. Pearlmann	*Morris Micklewhite and the Tangerine Dress* by C. Baldacchino
Gendered Expectations for Girls	*The Paper Bag Princess* by R. Munsch *Rosie Revere, Engineer* by A. Beaty *Not All Princesses Dress in Pink* by J. Yolen & H.Y. Stemple	*Drum Dream Girl* by M. Engle
Hair	*Long Hair, Don't Care* by J. Guerra *Hair Love* by M. Cherry *My Hair is a Garden* By C. Cabrera	*Don't Touch My Hair!* By S. Miller
Jewish Identity	*Queen of the Hanukkah Dosas* by P. Ehrenberg *Jalapeno Bagels* by N. Wing *Osnat and Her Dove* by S. Samuel	*Mrs. Katz and Tush* by P. Polacco

(Continued)

TABLE 2.2 (Continued)

Topic	Books That Affirm	Books That Demonstrate Struggle
Muslim Identity	*Amira's Picture Day* by A. Hussain *Deep in the Sahara* by K. Cunnane *Laila's Lunchbox* by R. Faruqi	*The Sandwich Swap* by R. Abdullah
Names	*Your Name is a Song* by J. Thompkins-Bigelow *Alma and How She Got Her Name* by J. Martinez-Neal *My Name is Sangoel* by K. Williams & K. Mohammed	*Thunder Boy Jr.* by S. Alexie
Palestinian Identity	*Homeland: My Father Dreams of Palestine* by H. Moushabeck *Halal Hot Dogs* by S. Aziz *P is for Palenstine: A Palestine Alphabet Book* by G. Bashi	*These Olive Trees* by A. Ghanameh
Persons with Disabilities	*I Get Around in My Own Special Way* by D. Goldman *Not So Different* – S. Burcaw *We're All Wonders* by R. J. Palacio	*Emmanuel's Dream* by L.A. Thompson
Racial Identity	*The Year We Learned to Fly* by J. Woodson *Black Boy Joy* by K. Mbalia *I Am Every Good Thing* by D. Barnes	*Something Happened In Our Town* by M. Celano & M. Collins
Skin Color	*All the Colors of the Earth* by S. Hamanaka *The Colors of Us* by K. Katz *The Skin You Live In* by M. Tyler	*Sulwe* by L. Nyong'o

TABLE 2.2 (Continued)

Topic	Books That Affirm	Books That Demonstrate Struggle
Socio-Economic Status	*Those Shoes* by M. Boelts *A Bike Like Sergio's* by M. Boelts *Last Stop on Market Street* by M. Pena	*¡Si, Se Puede! Yes, We Can! Janitor Strike in LA* by D. Cohn
Struggles with Literacy	*A Walk in the Words* by H. Talbott *The Wednesday Surprise* by E. Bunting *Mr. George Baker* by A. Hest	*Thank You, Mr. Falker* by P. Polacco

Helpful Online Resources

The following websites offer hundreds of titles that have been sorted in a variety of different ways to help you create critical text sets that meet the specific needs of your teaching.

Social Justice Books –

https://socialjusticebooks.org/booklists/

Equity thru Education –

https://www.equitythrued.com/ecel-text-sets

Worlds of Words –

https://wowlit.org/

Implementing Critical Text Sets into Our Instruction

Implementing critical text sets into our current teaching is rather straightforward, given the fact there isn't a single aspect of our literacy standards that cannot be taught through a carefully selected book or news article that invites students to think more deeply about issues of representation, equity, and justice. Furthermore, selecting these sorts of texts also allows us to integrate select social studies standards into our literacy instruction. For instance, many states have civics standards similar to the ones listed below.

> Identify similarities and differences between people and discuss ways to protect and respect all people by practicing civic dispositions.
>
> Apply history and social science skills to the content by: (1) recognizing cause and effect relationships, (2) developing questions, enhancing curiosity, and engaging in critical thinking and analysis, and (3) engaging and communicating as a civil and informed individual with persons with different perspectives.

By implementing critical text sets into literacy lessons about using multiple strategies when solving unknown words, retelling stories using a beginning, middle, and end, or developing practices that aid comprehension, we can help students begin to see how such skills help them gain greater access to information about a diversity of lived experiences, as well as the issues facing their communities. Let's see what this looks like in practice. While we draw on literacy standards from the state of South Carolina, this same literacy content can be found in standards across the nation.

Kindergarten

Standard	Critical Text Set	Classroom Practice
Literary Text 8.1 With guidance and support, read or listen closely to: a. describe characters and their actions; b. compare characters' experiences to those of the reader	**Topic:** Difference **Text Selection for This Lesson:** Mixed by A. Chung **Previously Read Identity-Affirming Books:** • All Are Welcome by A. Penfold • Where Are You From? by Y.S. Mendez • Eyes That Kiss at the Corners by J. Ho • This Is How We Do It: One Day in the Lives of Seven Kids Around the World by M. Lamothe	Before this mini-lesson, students will have already read a variety of texts throughout the year that focus on themes of difference and belonging. Students can start the year by listening to the book *All Are Welcome* and then exploring the diversity found within their own classroom before discussing the classroom norms they will develop to ensure everyone feels welcomed and cared for. Later in the year, they can read other titles that offer opportunities to celebrate differences in their hair and bodies as well as identify and celebrate the many different cultures and traditions represented in their classroom. For this particular lesson, Auree Chung's *Mixed* has been selected because the straightforward text and strong narrative elements lends themself perfectly to having students describe the different characters and draw connections between the story and their own experiences. In regard to integrating content that helps students become more aware of issues in their communities, this story about the reds, blues, and yellows all thinking they are the best and mistreating those who are different from themselves lends itself perfectly to a discussion about discrimination. Students can share their own stories of being mistreated based on how they look or act. It's critical here to bridge a story with fictional characters to real world examples. This discussion could take place during the reading, immediately after the reading, or the next day during Morning Meeting.

(Continued)

Second Grade

Standard	Critical Text Set	Classroom Practice
Informational Text 5.1 Ask and answer literal and inferential questions to demonstrate understanding of a text;	**Topic:** Cultural and Personal Significance of Names **Text Selection for This Lesson:** Name Discrimination Study Finds Lakisha And Jamal Still Less Likely To Get Hired Than Emily And Greg by R. Young & S. McMahon at WBUR News (https://www.wbur.org/hereandnow/2021/08/18/name-discrimination-jobs) **Previously Read Identity-Affirming Books:**<ul><li>*Alma and How She Got Her Name* by J. Martinez Neal</li><li>*Kantiga Finds the Perfect Name* by Mabel Mnensa</li><li>*Naming Ceremony* by S. Wedlick</li></ul>	Before this mini-lesson, students will have already read a variety of texts throughout the year that celebrate the cultural and personal significance of their names. For this particular lesson, a news article about name discrimination has been selected because it demonstrates evidence of unjust practices that will speak back to what they already learned about the cultural significance of names, which will elicit many questions about motives, oppressive beliefs, and violations of civil rights. Furthermore, there will be some parts of the article that will be somewhat difficult for students to immediately comprehend which will offer opportunities to demonstrate how readers ask questions of the text when they don't feel like they fully understand what they've read. In regard to integrating content that helps students become more aware of issues in their communities, this news article about a study showing that applicants with traditionally Black-sounding names are less likely to be called in for an interview, despite having comparable applications to those with traditionally white-sounding names, supports students to understand how discriminatory practices are deployed in the workforce. As the questions students are likely to ask will speak to the examples of injustice and inequity, they will learn how questions guide our reading while, simultaneously, thinking critically about discriminatory practices.

Fourth Grade

Standard	Critical Text Set	Classroom Practice
Literary Text Standard 8.1a Use text evidence to explain how conflicts cause the characters to change	**Topic:** Ableism **Text Selection for This Lesson:** *Emmanuel's Dream* by L.A. Thompson **Previously Read Identity-Affirming Books:** • *Not So Different: What You Really Want to Ask About Having a Disability* by S. Burcaw • *Tenacious: Fifteen Adventures Alongside Disabled Athletes* by P.C. Prevo • *London Marathon Gives Same Prize Money to Wheelchair Athletes* by J. Lederman & K. Brannelly at NBC News (https://www.nbcnews.com/news/sports/london-marathon-award-wheelchair-non-disabledd-athletes-equal-prize-mo-rcna148524)	Before this mini-lesson, students will have already read a variety of books and news articles that help them better understand the lived experiences of those living with disabilities, including numerous examples of people excelling physically, emotionally, and professionally. For this particular lesson, Laurie Ann Thompson's book, *Emmanuel's Dream*, was selected because this biographical account of Emmanuel Ofosu Yeboah's early life demonstrates how conflicts stemming from Ofosu Yeboah being born with one deformed leg served as a catalyst for his efforts to create change – both within himself and across the globe. Students can draw evidence from the text to support their claims when making connections between these conflicts and Ofosu Yeboah's actions. In regard to integrating content that helps students become more aware of issues in their communities, students are positioned to have a critical discussion about how various communities do or do not support and celebrate people with disabilities. The implementation of this text in the literacy block opens the door for future opportunities such as inviting guests into the classroom to share their own personal experiences with disability and having students go out into the community to gather data about accessibility at various buildings, parks, and gathering places.

As you can see, integrating a critical text set into your teaching can happen within a single unit (such as the second-grade exploration into names) or be stretched out over the course of a full year (as with the fourth-grade texts about persons with disabilities). There is no single best way of doing this work. That said, it's important to note that the most powerful learning happens when these themes and critical discussions return throughout the year in response to the many books and news articles that frame the work you do alongside your students during all parts of the day.

Classroom Examples

As you can see, when we are intentional in the choices we make, integrating current news and issues into our literacy practices is a rather natural process. We will now provide a few examples showing how classroom teachers have implemented these practices into their own teaching. The first example shows how fourth-grade teacher Tianna Myers uses the morning meeting to revisit a news article from their literacy block so students can discuss a law allowing teachers to carry firearms at school. The second example features a kindergarten teacher, Alexa Weeks, as she uses critical text sets to support the work her students do as readers and writers throughout the day.

Fourth Graders Discuss the Merits of a Law Allowing Teachers to Carry a Concealed Weapon

In addition to requiring her students to share one journal entry and one current news article in their morning meeting each month, Tianna Myers also embeds current news articles into her literacy instruction and then occasionally brings these articles back to the class a second time during the next day's morning meeting. This provides them with extended time to explore the issues that emerge from these texts. In the following vignette, the class has already read a news article about Tennessee passing a law that allows classroom teachers to carry concealed weapons at school. Having used this article the day before as part of their literacy instruction, they now turn their attention to analyzing the law based on their own knowledge, experiences, hopes, and concerns.

TIANNA: So having read the article yesterday, I'm curious – do you agree? Will this make schools safer?

CASON: I think it would deter some things but I don't feel like it's the safest option. The safest option would be just hiring more SROs or more security people or high tech surveillance cameras or something.

COLTON: What's the difference between having open carry or having a concealed gun?

TIANNA: So, having concealed means people can't see it like if it's in your purse or bag but open carry is when it's on your hip. It's in the open where people can see you're carrying it.

IAN: Like with police officers.

AMY: My dad is a police officer and sometimes when we go to a restaurant he puts his shirt over his gun in case others might be uncomfortable. So, it's concealed I guess.

TREY: If I had one, I would want it concealed because I don't want people looking at me weird. Based on my thoughts, when I'm around somebody with a gun I don't necessarily feel the safest.

TIANNA: So what do you feel about teachers being able to carry concealed weapons?

ELIZABETH: I think that would sort of make me feel unsafe because what if the teacher goes rogue or something? What if they get angry or something?

SAMMY: I think there should be more training than like 40 hours. A lot more training.

TERRI: I agree with Elizabeth. I just feel like this might not be the right thing to do. I feel like there could be something different people could do because it could get used in the wrong way or something could go wrong.

TIANNA: I think my fear is not that teachers would go rogue because we learn how to handle frustration really well because it's an important part of our jobs. My worry is that when I decided to become a teacher, I didn't expect to be carrying a gun. I didn't go to school for that. That's not a responsibility I want to take on.

XAVIER: I also worry that a kid might get the gun. That's a concern I have. I personally feel like we should hire more security if that's what we need. Because there might be an accident and I don't like that feeling at all.

TREY: I think especially with older kids – like eighth grade and above – that could happen. I just feel like it would be older kids because they would do that stuff. Take the gun.

TIANNA: I hear what you're saying but there was a story a year or two ago about a first grader in Virginia who shot their teacher.

XAVIER: There are also stories about kids our age who have brought weapons to school – or tried to bring weapons to school. I feel like it might be a stereotype to say it's older kids because some younger kids have done it too. We shouldn't say older kids are bad because we'll be older kids and we won't be bad. We don't want people saying that about us.

Izzy: And aren't younger kids more impressionable or willing to do things they see on TV shows?

Tianna: So we've heard lots of concerns but I'm wondering if anyone is thinking this could be a positive thing? Could it be safer to have teachers with guns?

Colton: I think it could make it safer. It would just have to have lots of precautions and maybe a smaller gun. I think it should be a sidearm. Not a peashooter, but something that's enough to keep people safe.

Cason: I just feel like there would have to be a lot of safety – like a safety mode and a holster that covers the trigger.

Amy: And maybe there could be technology where only their fingerprint can make the gun work. Then kids couldn't use it.

Colton: Can you do that?

Sammy: Probably, because scientists are doing a lot. They could probably do that. We have fingerprint locks on phones.

For her part, Tianna selects an article that explores a timely topic, integrates this text into her literacy instruction, and then facilitates a morning meeting discussion where kids feel comfortable speaking openly – even when disagreeing with their teacher. This work lies at the heart of preparing young children for greater civic engagement.

Kindergartners Use Critical Text Sets to Support Their Growth as Readers and Writers

When Alexa Weeks began considering ways to help her kindergarten students become aware of important issues, she

Voices from the Classroom

Ian Johnson

"In Ms. Myer's class, most days we would see the news and we would have discussions about it. Sometimes our discussions would go into serious topics like the border and those kinds of things. I like that my teachers really listened to us and respected our opinions. Sometimes people underestimate children just because they are young but they also have a lot of important perspectives to share....There were some times when I heard something someone shared and I kind of changed my mind – maybe a point I hadn't thought about. I liked to play devil's advocate with my own thoughts, too, and ask myself, 'Why do you actually believe this? Is it because of something in the media or my parent's thoughts, but not my own thoughts?' Everybody has these things that they maybe just believe but they're not actually true".

– Ian (now reflecting on his experiences in elementary school)

had to be strategic. Like so many other teachers across the country, her district placed strict mandates on her teaching in regard to what literacy instruction should look like and exactly how her time should be spent. Her first thought was to begin this work during the class' Morning Meeting. However, yet another district expectation demanded that she deliver guidance lessons during this time of day. It felt as though nearly every single minute was being taken away by prescriptive programs and resources.

In preparation for the work she wanted to do, Alexa collected critical texts on topics she knew she could use to celebrate her students' social identities as they entered their first year of formal schooling. She also wanted these texts to help her students think more carefully about how they treat students within their classroom and school. The titles she selected included books about hair, skin color, names, gendered expectations, diverse family structures, and multilingualism. After some thought, Alexa realized she could use these books to explore important issues while simultaneously teaching mandated guidance topics such as friendship, bullying, cultural awareness, and determination. Integration provided the perfect solution.

Over the course of the year, she developed multi-week inquiries based on the critical text sets she had collected. After taking a few weeks to get the kids settled into their new classroom and routines, the first topic they explored was the cultural and personal significance of their names. Alexa dedicated ten to fifteen minutes of her morning meeting to reading books together and learning to have discussions that connected their own experiences, feelings, and needs to what they were learning. She also sent her students home to interview family members about the origins of their names and provided time in the morning meeting for each of the children to share what they had learned. Afterward, Alexa helped them create a class book about their names. Once it was finished, she made multiple copies and sent them home with the children so they could read the class-authored text to their families. Finally, drawing on the discussions that filled the room during this exploration, Alexa concluded the study with a reading of Kevin Henkes' book, *Chrysanthemum*. In the story, a young mouse arrives for her first day of kindergarten only to be mercilessly teased about the length and meaning of her name. This book positioned the students to reflect on the importance of honoring all people's names and discuss what they could do if they ever heard someone around them being mistreated in such a way.

While this work took place within Morning Meeting, Alexa was deliberate in ensuring these engagements would support her students' literacy learning. Over the course of 3 weeks, she uncovered many of her oral language, reading, and writing standards such as: increasing literacy and speaking vocabulary, relating previous experiences to what is read, using pictures to make predictions, asking and answering questions about what is read, printing their names, and using letters and beginning consonant sounds to phonetically spell words.

As the year progressed, Alexa began integrating these critical text sets into her literacy block as well. For instance, she found she could use these stories when teaching whole class, comprehension mini-lessons, or when working with small groups. In doing so, she refused to allow rigid mandates to bar her from the work she knew her kids and community needed most.

In each of these examples, we see classroom teachers making intentional moves to help their students become aware of issues within the classroom, school, and community. This is critical work, as students in these types of classrooms are much more likely to grow into adults who are well-informed and who care about those within, and beyond, their community. In the next chapter, we'll discuss how to support students to engage in productive dialogue around these issues.

CHAPTER 3

Helping Students Engage in Critical Discussion

TEACHER: Ok, so in this article a student, DeAndre, was barred from his high school graduation because the school said his dreadlocks were against the dress code. What do you notice?

COLBY: My mom told me dress codes were so people wouldn't get distracted. But I feel like this one about his hair is for a bad reason. I feel like this is for a different reason.

TEACHER: What do you think that reason might be?

BLAIZE: Racism.

COLBY: I just know distracting isn't the reason.

TJ: Well, his hair was important because it was about his family and his life.

TEACHER: You mean, because the article explained that generations of men in his family wore their hair that same way?

TJ: Yeah, his family had dreadlocks. It was part of their culture but he wasn't allowed to do it at school.

BLAIZE: That's not fair!

There was a time in our earliest days of teaching when we (Katie, Lester, and Chris) falsely assumed young children weren't prepared to talk about tough issues like racism, sexism, or homophobia. To be honest, even if we *had* been aware of our students' readiness, we may not have felt prepared to have classroom discussions like the one above about a racist school policy. This takes time. Our comfort and skill to navigate these conversations is ever evolving.

One of our biggest issues was the fact there really weren't many models at that time for what critical discussions should look like in an elementary classroom. Fortunately, teachers today have professional texts such as Sonja Cherry-Paul's *Antiracist Reading Revolution* (2024), Matthew Kay and Jennifer Orr's *We're Gonna Keep on Talking* (2023), and Chris' *Social Justice Talk* (2020) that provide a vision for how these discussions might go, as well as offer support to get teachers started. But it's not just us that needs a vision and support for this work – it's our students, too. We shouldn't assume the children in our classrooms have had many positive examples of critical discussion in "mixed company" – either in or out of the classroom. Think back to your own childhood. How did holiday dinners go once people started debating politics? If it went smoothly, consider yourself lucky because there are a whole host of shows, movies, and late-night comedy sketches that suggest most of us have seen discussions about politics and social issues go sideways very quickly.

It's very possible the same is true of our students. The only times they may have seen these discussions take place is during a heated argument among relatives or when stumbling upon bits and pieces of toxic behavior on social media, the internet, or in the news. If our students are to become meaningfully engaged – developing empathy and compassion for those around them, staying abreast of important issues, and taking action – it's important that they learn to engage in productive discussion while evaluating multiple perspectives.

While positive models for what these discussions can look like are helpful, there are other issues to consider as well. For many teachers, the most troubling issue is the fact that efforts to address injustice or inequity in the classroom are oftentimes attacked by school boards, legislators, and certain corners of the national media, as politicized debates rage on about what should or should not be taught in public school classrooms. Yet, it's important to recognize that such attacks aren't new. We have *long* been mired in challenging times for discussions around racism, oppression, and injustice. Kay and Orr (2023) write,

> This is not the first time that teaching the truth has been unpopular, or that authentic analysis of 'controversial' topics has been legislated against … We teachers of good will need more than a general understanding of this history; we need to collect this history like fuel. Bad actors have tried all of this before – and they have failed because of the righteous stubbornness of teachers just like us.
>
> (pp. 6–7)

Drawing inspiration from these words, we must invest ourselves in becoming righteously stubborn teachers who refuse to allow bad actors to stop us from working alongside our students to create a more just tomorrow. In this chapter, we will discuss specific steps teachers can take to support students in rich dialogue. But first, let's explore a few key points that are integral to this work. These include: when and where these discussions can take place in our classrooms, the importance of allowing ourselves and those around us to make mistakes, and the reasons why students sometimes choose to disengage from sensitive topics.

Conversation, Discussion, and Debate: What's the Difference?

There are many specific terms that are used to describe the nature of talk for different purposes. Let's take a moment to define some of these and consider which most accurately represents the work we are doing alongside students as we engage with important topics and look for opportunities to take action.

Conversation is a casual exchange of stories, ideas, feelings, etc. We often see students having conversations throughout the day as they talk about their lives, favorite games, and so on. For instance, in the vignette at the top of the chapter, students could have engaged in conversation by simply sharing stories about their own hairstyles or maybe even telling stories about times people had disapproved of their hair.

Discussion is an interchange of ideas that is meant to build a greater understanding of a specific topic. There is a goal of reaching some sort of mutual understanding by the end of the discussion – even if that mutual understanding is the recognition of multiple perspectives from which the topic can be viewed. The students in the classroom above were having a discussion because they were actively analyzing (why did this happen) and critiquing (was this fair) what had happened while building a better understanding of how racist beliefs can shape school policies.

Debate is an oppositional interchange of facts and ideas where each speaker is working to defend their own position on a given topic. Participants listen to one another so that they can formulate counterarguments to defend their own position. The aim of a debate is to win. If the discussion above were framed as a debate, the teacher would have had groups prepare and deliver arguments in favor of or against the presence of school policies that address student appearance.

In this book, the work we are describing comes in the form of classroom discussion. Our aim is to create classroom spaces where students have the opportunity to share while listening to peers who may offer different experiences, perspectives, and knowledge. The goal in these discussions is not to win, but to work toward developing a better, and more nuanced, understanding of important topics.

When and Where Critical Discussions Take Place

A common misconception is that teachers must develop whole new structures or carve out specific, stand-alone times in their weekly schedule for students to discuss current events and issues. We see this approach put into action when well-meaning teachers devote one weekly morning meeting to current news, stage a weekly discussion around a predetermined issue, or develop a debate unit that will scaffold students into exploring an issue from multiple perspectives. While these are great places to begin, we shouldn't limit our students to isolated opportunities to think critically about the communities in which they live. The rigorous work students do to comprehend, analyze, and critique multimodal texts (including newspaper articles, news clips, biographies, picture books, videos, print advertisements, speeches, and songs) not only helps them grow stronger literacy skills but addresses many of the state standards teachers are tasked with teaching in the first place (see Table 3.1).

What Does This Mean for Our Teaching?

We must be intentional in creating multiple opportunities throughout the week for students to engage in critical dialogue. We do this by implementing thought-provoking texts, such as the critical text sets provided in Chapter 2, into our

TABLE 3.1

Sample Literacy Standards at Work When Critically Reading and Discussing Texts

Explore topics of interest to formulate logical questions; build knowledge; generate possible explanations; consider alternative views.
Ask and answer literal and inferential questions to determine meaning; refer explicitly to the text to support inferences and conclusions.
Summarize multi-paragraph texts using key details to support the central idea.
Use paragraph-level context to determine the meaning of words and phrases.
Compare and contrast diverse texts on the same topic, idea, or concept.
State the author's purpose; distinguish one's own perspective from that of the author.
Describe the structures an author uses to support specific points.
Read and respond according to task and purpose to become self-directed, critical readers and thinkers.

daily teaching. These texts can be incorporated into any subject area and then used to scaffold students into sharing connections, posing questions, and offering critique. Doing this work on a consistent basis provides young learners the opportunity to accumulate shared knowledge they can draw upon, both individually and collectively, during future discussions.

To create multiple opportunities for these discussions throughout the week, we also need to incorporate rich discussions into different parts of the school day. Doing so ensures we are looking at issues through multiple lenses (i.e. as a reader, writer, social scientist, scientist, and mathematician). Furthermore, it removes the burden of trying to make all of this work fit within a single subject (say, just in reading or in social studies). Table 3.2 demonstrates how Tianna Myers, who loops with her students from fourth to fifth grade, invites her students into critical discussion throughout the school week.

TABLE 3.2
Providing Opportunity for Critical Dialogue Throughout the School Day

Daily Structure	Tianna's Fifth-Grade Classroom
Morning Meeting	Tianna begins each and every day with a morning meeting that invites students to share things they've been noticing or thinking, framing these as a question that invites their classmates into discussion (i.e. "Why do all the dollar bills have men on them?" or "Why does so much stuff wind up in the trash when it should be recycled?") The student asking the question then facilitates the discussion, calling on classmates and making connections to what has been shared. In addition to student questions, Tianna also requires her students to share one news article with the class each month. After each student provides a summary of their article, Tianna invites their peers into discussion by asking, "What are you thinking?" or "What questions or comments do you have?" By having her students share observations, questions, and news articles each morning, there is not a single day of the school year when students do not engage in rich discussion around a topic of their choosing. Some topics are critical in nature while others are not. No matter, each discussion provides students an opportunity to learn how to build productive dialogue.

(*Continued*)

TABLE 3.2 (Continued)

Daily Structure	Tianna's Fifth-Grade Classroom
Literacy	Because Tianna regularly uses texts that address a wide variety of issues (such as identity, diversity, and injustice), she is deliberate in teaching her students to make connections, ask questions, and draw conclusions that help promote rich dialogue as well as a deeper understanding of the text. To do this, Tianna is careful not to rush her students through instruction, focusing only on the academic knowledge and skills being taught. Rather, she builds time into her lessons for students to engage in purposeful conversations about their thinking, share out important ideas with the class, and invite their peers into collaborative meaning making. In doing so, Tianna supports her students to become more engaged readers who understand the role texts play in helping us think more critically about the world around us.
Social Studies	In social studies, Tianna supports her students to think critically about the content in their state standards and textbooks, particularly in regard to whose stories are being memorialized and what impact this can have on students learning about history. One quick way to launch this discussion is to have students skim each chapter and pay attention to the illustrations and photographs to determine which social groups are being placed at the forefront. Additionally, Tianna regularly invites her students into discussion about the nature of primary and secondary resources as a lens for critiquing historical accounts. These themes (what are we supposed to learn, what does the text include and exclude, and are these accounts coming from reliable sources) provide opportunities for important discussions within each unit of study.
Science	In science, Tianna draws on the scientific method when calling on students to observe and then generate and analyze various hypotheses. The support she provides students as they engage in analytical thinking supports the other discussions that happen across the school day.

TABLE 3.2 (Continued)

Daily Structure	Tianna's Fifth-Grade Classroom
Math	In math, Tianna regularly has students share strategies they have developed to solve problems and then uses these to invite classmates into discussion about the nature of mathematical concepts, the relationships between numbers, and the role of flexible thinking when encountering new problems.

The Importance of Making Mistakes

Because engaging in critical discussion calls on each of us to speak from our current understanding of a variety of topics, it's inevitable that we will not always say the right thing. Mistakes will be made. Yet, as much as we want our students to understand that making mistakes is a natural part of learning, we often do not afford ourselves (or, at times, those around us) this same margin of error when it comes to talking about issues that center on social identity. This is because so much of our own identities – particularly, how we'd like those within the community to see us – is wrapped up in whether or not we've said the *right* thing. But we must shift our thinking around this. We cannot reach our potential for growth if we aren't willing to speak honestly and remain open to others helping us interrogate our own beliefs and assumptions. We must be committed to critical reflection and a willingness to say, "I used to think…but now I'm realizing…" The same is true for our students.

What Does This Mean for Our Teaching?

Of course, this difficult work can only happen when we've made great strides to build a community of trust where students have genuine respect and appreciation for one another; so much so that a miscue during a class discussion is not an indictment on their character but a welcomed opportunity for growth. Teachers already do many wonderful things to build this sort of community – inviting students to share pieces of their homelives, welcoming families into the classroom, creating lots of opportunities for collaboration, reading books that promote respect and care, and celebrating individual and collective student successes, to name just a few. But while a strong sense of community in the classroom is vital to maximizing the potential of these discussions, we must also demonstrate the importance of being vulnerable. We must show our students that we've all had moments in our lives when our thinking wasn't quite where it needed to be. In truth, we're living in such a moment right now, as the path toward greater enlightenment spans a lifetime.

A powerful example of this happened during a discussion in Chris' third-grade classroom about the fact women made up less than 30% of their state legislature. One of his students asked her classmates why there were so few women at the State House. The class hypothesized that women may have been dissuaded from running, may not have seen a lot of other women doing this and assumed it wasn't for them, or didn't have people willing to provide the funds needed to run an expensive campaign. After a few minutes of discussion, one of the boys offered his own analysis: "I think it's because men are just better at it than women". Shocked by this statement, the circle erupted into chaos as many people started talking over one another in an effort to put the offending student in his place. To head off the anger and move the discussion in a more productive direction, Chris jumped in to demonstrate the fact he'd made a similar mistake in his own thinking which became an opportunity to grow.

CHRIS: I can understand how someone might think this – that men are better leaders than women. It's completely false, of course. In fact, it couldn't be any further from the truth because we see so many examples of strong female leaders doing great things. But when I was little I didn't notice those women as much as I should have. What I saw was that all the church ministers were men, and all the presidents were men, and all the sports coaches I watched were men, and – as we've been discussing now – that so many of our elected officials were men. Because of this, I just assumed that was the way it was supposed to be. I want to say that I'm embarrassed to have thought such a thing but, in all honesty, I wasn't given many opportunities to have people challenge me for that sort of thinking. It wasn't something that was discussed at school, or in my home. That's why I'm so glad we have these discussions here, because all of us – every single one of us – likely believes something about a group of people that is false. But when we share those things here in the group, we allow ourselves to make mistakes that lead to growth – to know better. And it makes sense that these things can make some of us angry to hear. No one wants to be disrespected. So, I'd like to thank you all for being brave enough to make mistakes, and for being kind enough to allow those around you to make their own mistakes too. That's how we grow.

Understanding Why Students Choose to Disengage

The fear of saying the wrong thing is emblematic of a multitude of reasons why people, including young children, avoid discussions around sensitive topics.

Sociologists Amy Lusk and Adam Weinberg (1994) identify three primary reasons students disengage from these types of classroom discussions. These include:

- concerns for preserving their relationships with peers,
- discomfort disagreeing with the teacher, and
- apprehension about navigating the social politics (i.e. power dynamics) that are at play among students in the classroom.

In the dissertation research Chris conducted in his second and third-grade classroom, he defined these barriers in even greater detail, finding that his seven-, eight-, and nine-year-old students sometimes disengaged because: (1) they didn't feel they had enough background knowledge to speak confidently, (2) they feared inviting conflict, (3) they didn't want to risk hurting friends by saying the wrong thing, and (4) they were uncomfortable hearing hard truths about the world they live in (Hass, 2020).

What Does This Mean for Our Teaching?

Before conducting his research, Chris had spent years telling people that children were largely immune from these tensions – that they openly invited opportunities to explore issues of fairness, kindness, and justice. It wasn't until he asked his students to reflect on the nature of these discussions that he discovered he had been operating from a false assumption – holding on to a belief that he *wanted* to be true rather than actually inquiring to find out.

As facilitators of these discussions, we need to know why some students disengage so that we can better support them in discussion. To do this, we provide prompts such as:

Tell me how you're feeling about our class discussions about [insert topic].

What have you learned?

What do you appreciate most about these discussions?

What's been a challenge?

Are there times you don't want to share your thoughts? Why?

How can we help one another feel more comfortable sharing?

The reflective discussions that grow out of this line of questioning invite opportunities for both the teacher and the students to develop new perspectives and helpful strategies to better navigate critical discussion. Furthermore, when we call on students to think metacognitively about their own participation and then invite them to become part of the process of analyzing, evaluating, and revising the nature of this work, they are far more likely to see it as genuine and invest themselves fully.

Secondly, we need to work proactively to implement classroom practices that scaffold students into success. Table 3.3 describes a number of practices that teachers have found to be helpful in their own classrooms.

TABLE 3.3
Strategies to Support Student Engagement

Barrier to Engagement	What Can We Do?	How Do We Do It?
Lacks the background knowledge to contribute	Provide opportunities for students to share their thinking with a neighbor before asking anyone to contribute to the whole group	While students will develop a significant amount of background knowledge over the course of the year as we read and discuss lots of texts, some may still feel less comfortable with their developing understanding of a topic. For this reason, before asking our students to share out to a larger group, we afford them the opportunity to first try out their thinking with a partner as part of a turn-and-talk. Not only does this allow them to think through what they might share later, but it also provides them an opportunity to hear someone else's ideas – which may bolster or shape their own current thinking.
Wary of conflict	Explicitly teach students the value of disagreement and how to navigate it	As will be discussed later in this chapter, we can diffuse much of the fear students feel about disagreement by helping them better understand why debate can be an important tool in allowing us to more fully understand a topic. We can also help them learn what type of language is most productive when disagreeing, as well as the effects of our body language and tone.

TABLE 3.3 (Continued)

Barrier to Engagement	What Can We Do?	How Do We Do It?
Fearful of saying something hurtful	Set expectations for how we respond to someone when they share something hurtful and then model what this looks like	Just as we help students understand the importance of disagreement, we must help them understand that some perspectives may feel hurtful to us and that we have the right to speak up and help our classmates understand this. The trick here is to give them the language that is more likely to invite peers to listen, rather than becoming defensive or shutting down. When we model this for students, we may use strategies such as: (1) framing the miscue as an opportunity to grow, (2) sharing our own history of faulty thinking to diffuse the situation, (3) identifying the larger social forces at play that promote such thinking, and (4) inviting them to revise what they just said to better reflect their thinking (Hass, 2020). For instance, we might say to someone who has made a hurtful remark about same-sex couples, "We know there are many different types of families in this world – and in this classroom. Every single one of us has someone in this world who loves us very much. But while our families might look different from one another in some ways, they are all incredibly special. So, can you think about how you might make that last statement differently?"

(Continued)

TABLE 3.3 (Continued)

Barrier to Engagement	What Can We Do?	How Do We Do It?
Uncomfortable hearing hard truths	Carefully determine what is and is not appropriate for our students; Balance negative examples with heavy doses of positive examples to help students feel they are safe and cared for	Just as the critical text sets offered students multiple opportunities to celebrate social identities and to highlight positive things happening in people's everyday lives before delving into a critique of oppressive beliefs and practices, we must temper critical discussions during any part of the school day with stories of hope and cheer. For one, this provides a healthy balance. Secondly, this allows our students opportunities to decompress, to leave these issues alone for a while so that they'll be better situated to tackle them later. Thirdly, we should always be thinking very carefully about what topics would be appropriate for our students and which should not. This isn't to say that we avoid talking about school shootings, racist policies, or harmful stereotypes. It just means that we are mindful in selecting which individual examples of these issues are shared with the class – especially given the fact some topics can be triggering or traumatic for certain students. This speaks to the importance of really getting to know our students so we can make responsible choices and navigate classroom engagements with care.

Once Chris learned the error he made in assuming kids felt comfortable, he began facilitating check-ins throughout the year to learn what his students were thinking in response to the nature of their critical discussions. In the following vignette, Chris invites his third graders to share any tensions that might affect their participation in critical discussions.

CHRIS: So, we've been having some pretty important discussions in our morning meeting the past couple of months. People have put lots of things in our journals for us to discuss. Some have been in the science journal about how dams make electricity or why worms come out after it rains. Others have come from the classroom community journal about things we do in the classroom that are kind but also things that sometimes make it hard to feel safe, or even feel happy. Some have been in the culture journal and have challenged us to think about issues related to race and gender and religion and living with a disability, and other things like that. I'm wondering, how do those discussions, the ones in the culture journal, make you feel? Do you think they've been going well? Is there ever anything that makes you uncomfortable or maybe even unsure about whether or not you should share out loud? Ronald?

RONALD: Sometimes I feel uncomfortable.

CHRIS: Okay, that's helpful to know. Why is that, do you think?

RONALD: Because I was afraid I might say the wrong thing. Yeah, because one time, I don't mean no offense Derrick but...

DERRICK: No offense bro.

RONALD: one time Derrick accidentally said the wrong thing and everyone was like "Derrick!"

DERRICK: Yeah!

CHRIS: What was it, Derick? Do you remember?

DERRICK: I'm not sure but every time, most of the time when the boys say something wrong, the girls are like "Ahhhh!"

CHRIS: Sarah, what did you want to say?

SARAH: Well, because I play soccer and I also play football with my older cousin and I think if somebody says something like "boys are more athletic" it'll hurt my feelings because I do a lot of sports too.

CHRIS: Silas?

SILAS: I thought it was a little uncomfortable sometimes because I don't want to say the wrong thing or I don't want to offend someone and they're going to get mad. I don't want to hurt anyone's feelings. And it's like I would be really uncomfortable if I did say something wrong and I don't want to do that again. So I'm just a little uncomfortable because in a few discussions I knew I'd say something that probably would offend someone so I decided not to say it. So I felt uncomfortable.

CHRIS: Wow, these are really important thoughts you all are sharing. Thanks for being so honest and for being brave enough to share your feelings. I know that's not always real easy. So, I'm wondering – what should we do with this information? Can we maybe take each of these points one at a time and think about strategies for helping ourselves and our classmates feel more comfortable sharing their thoughts – especially knowing that we might sometimes need others in the classroom to help us think about something in a new way?

In providing space for students to share openly and honestly, Chris not only acknowledged their feelings but also provided an opportunity to use his students' experiences as a catalyst for new learning, while also supporting them to build stronger relationships with one another built on mutual trust and care.

Now that we have an understanding of where these discussions can take place in our classrooms, the importance of giving grace when working to outgrow faulty thinking, and the reasons why students sometimes choose to disengage from sensitive topics, let's explore how you can begin supporting your students into meaningful discussion.

Not Sure Where to Begin? Try This...

First off, it's important to note that not every single discussion needs to be critical in nature. All classroom talk is important because it provides an opportunity to support students in productive dialogue. When we are deliberate in our practices, we can use any classroom discussion as an opportunity to teach students to engage in empathetic listening (as discussed in Chapter 1), build upon shared ideas, and challenge those things that seem to lack adequate logic or truth. In this section, we detail how class discussion can grow directly from our students' observations and questions, ways we can improve the quality of discussion, and ideas for extending these discussions into our students' homes so their families can be part of this work.

Make Discussion a Consistent Component of Daily Learning

Engaging students in discussion is essential. Classroom discussion provides students with opportunities to construct new knowledge (Vygotsky, 1962) rather than passively receiving it (Freere, 2000). When we root our teaching in class discussion, students are positioned to be agentive; to take ownership of their learning. One way they do this is by asking lots of questions. A teacher friend of ours, Tim O'Keefe, once told a story about a student in his classroom whose father asked the same question each and every night – *What questions did you ask today?* Not How *was school?* or *What did you play during recess?* (though he may have asked those as well), but *What questions did you ask today?* In doing so, this father created a daily expectation that school is a place for asking questions. He also helped his child build an identity as someone who would regularly ask those important questions. In this section, we'll explore how student questions, as well as their observations, can be a catalyst for daily discussion.

Using Student Questions to Fuel Classroom Discussion

When we think about building classroom practices that are deeply rooted in discussion, a great place to begin is by creating space for students to share their questions. While this is a simple practice, it's quite powerful. To do this, we pause and tell our kids, "Hey, I want you to turn to someone right now and tell them what you're wondering about. What questions do you have about [this story, this graph, this video, this historical text, etc]?" At the beginning, our students might not have many questions. In fact, it's very likely that you might see a room full of absent stares and indifferent shrugs. But over time, students will begin to anticipate this practice. Because it happens so regularly, they will know you have an expectation that each and every one of them will have important questions to ask because they're listening carefully and thinking deeply. And just like that child's father, you will help them develop new identities for themselves as learners who ask great questions and then invite those around them into discussion in search of answers.

Notice that we said they invite *those* around them into discussion. That's because these questions are posed to the entire class – not just the teacher. As a result, our students' questions become a catalyst for small-group and whole-group discussion. Let's take a look at how this might sound across various parts of the school day.

	Context	Teacher Prompting	Ensuing Discussion
Morning Meeting	A student has just shared a news article about a group of people in a small town who are fighting to stop their Muslim neighbors from building a larger mosque.	"So, it sounds like the Muslim community wants to build a mosque but quite a few people in this town are fighting against it. They're protesting, burning flags, shouting. Before we begin our discussion, I'm curious…what are you wondering? What questions do you have? Is anything here that's not making sense to you? Turn and share with a neighbor".	In each case, students have the opportunity to share their own questions and thoughts with a partner or write about them in a journal before bringing these back to the whole group. This not only provides them an opportunity to prepare for what they might say later but also gives each and every child an outlet for their thinking – which is a tremendous way to increase engagement and critical thinking. As the class returns to the whole group, two or three students are called on to share before asking if
Literacy	The teacher has just finished reading Jacqueline Woodson's book *Each Kindness*. In the story, one of the main characters, Chloe, joins with her friends in mistreating a new student at school. By the time Chloe decides to make amends for her harmful behavior, she finds out it is too late, as the student has already moved away.	"Throughout the book we've seen Chloe and her friends ignore and ridicule Maya. When Chloe is finally ready to do better, to maybe apologize, it's too late. Tell me, what are you wondering? What questions do you have about the story, the characters, the ending? When you're ready, turn and talk with a neighbor. Tell them what you're wondering and see if the two of you can make some sense of your questions".	

	Context	Teacher Prompting	Ensuing Discussion
Math	While studying how to read and analyze tables and graphs, the class is presented with data showing how safe (or unsafe) people feel when there is a gun in their house.	"This is interesting because the gun owners feel quite a bit safer having a gun in the house, but other people in the house – those who don't actually own the gun – were less likely to say the gun made them feel safe. Hmmm, what are you wondering? What questions do you have? Take a moment to think about this and in just a moment I'll have you turn and talk with a partner to build a discussion around your questions".	anyone has anything to add. In this way, students are tasked with co-creating curriculum alongside us as their questions and thoughts become the backbone of classroom discussion.
Science	While studying how animals adapt to their environment, the class watches a video about problematic bear activity near a national park.	"It looks like the bears are adapting, right? They're starting to seek out food from the people, instead of nature. There's a lot going on here. What are you wondering? When you think about what's happening with these bears and the people in the parks, what questions do you have? Take a moment to record a question or two in your science journal and in just a minute I'll have you turn to your partner to discuss".	

(Continued)

	Context	Teacher Prompting	Ensuing Discussion
Social Studies	During a study of Colonial America, the class finds a table stating there were just 200 people living in their state in 1670; yet, online research reveals there would have been thousands of Native Americans living there during that same time.	"So we have two different numbers – one says 200 people lived in our state and the other says it's in the thousands. Hmmm, I'm a little confused and I bet some of you are too. Tell me, what are you wondering? What questions do you have? Take a moment to jot a few sentences into your journal. Share your questions as well as what you're thinking about these. In about five minutes, you'll have a chance to turn and share with someone".	

Using Student Observations to Fuel Classroom Discussion

In addition to using student questions to fuel classroom discussion, we can also build student-centered discussions by asking children to share their observations. This practice calls on students to consider what they've just read, viewed, or heard and then identify what stood out as particularly important to them. We frame this by asking, "What do you notice?" (Mills, 2014).

Rather than confining student thought with a closed-ended question or prompt that limits their thinking, the open-ended nature of "What do you notice?" allows space for students to co-construct curriculum alongside us as they notice and name aspects of the text that feel most important to them and then build a discussion around this. As with asking students what questions they have, this is a practice that ensures our teaching is responsive to student interests, tensions, and needs. Also, this practice positions our students to be active readers who pay careful attention to their thinking as they move through a text.

To illustrate what this looks like in practice, let's take a look at a third grade classroom where students have just finished reading *I Am Not a Number* by Jenny Kay Dupuis and Kathy Kacer (2016). In this story, Dupuis, a member of the Nipissing First Nation, recounts the story of her grandmother being forcefully placed in a residential school meant to "civilize" her and other Indigenous children by stripping them of their culture. In the afterword, she explains that many children were physically abused at these schools and some even died.

TEACHER: That was a powerful story. Let's just sit silently for a moment and think about what we just heard. In just a moment, I'm going to ask you: What were you noticing about this story? What were you thinking as you imagined all these things happening in your head? What is it you want us to talk about?

[students sit silently for about thirty seconds]

TEACHER: Rachel?

RACHEL: I was noticing that the people at the school were really mean to her.

JAKE: Yeah, they didn't even let her talk to her brother.

RACHEL: Or use her own name.

ZEKE: Yeah, they called her 750. That's so rude!

MICHELLE: No, it was 759.

TEACHER: Why do you think that was? Why might they have done these things?

IMANI: I think it's because they don't like her tribe.

RACHEL: I don't think they like any tribe, probably.

JAKE: They're probably racist.

TEACHER: Why do you say that?

JAKE: Because they were being mean to her and telling her to rub the brown off when she was washing in the sink.

ALEXIS: That's so wrong.

ELLA: Did she mean the dirt or her skin.

ALEXIS: She meant her skin!

IMANI: They also burned her hands when she tried to share her food.

DONALD: Because she wasn't speaking English.

TEACHER: So people are saying racism is what led the people at this school to treat children this way. But the government was involved too, right? They were the ones who said children had no say. Families had no say. They had to go.

JAKE: Like when the guy came to get her and her brother and they hid in the shed.

TEACHER: Is there anything else? What else did you notice?

DONALD: I liked how her family hid her. Her dad could have gotten in trouble.

RACHEL: Yeah, they were going to take him to jail I think.

TEACHER: That's a great point. Her family had to make a hard decision.

JAKE: Wouldn't be hard for me. I wouldn't be going to that school.

TEACHER: Fair enough. Maybe not so hard because you want to protect your family.

> But hard if someone has to go to jail and you can't see them. One thing I love about this book is that it shows how the family fought back. There's another story about these schools but it was written by a white woman, instead of someone from the actual tribe. In her version, the families don't fight back. They say the school might be helpful to their son.

DONALD: What?!

TEACHER: Yeah, they say to get ahead in this world it will be important to speak English and know how white people act. A lot of people felt like the book should have also shown the Cheyenne people fighting back. They could have learned English without being treated that way. Without being stripped of their culture. That's one of the problems when someone writes about another group's history. So, growing off of your discussion, I'm wondering: do schools still do this, do you think? Do they still try to change students? To make them all the same?

In this discussion, students play a key role in determining what is important, determining what is discussed, and creating meaning from the story. The role of the teacher is to facilitate – keeping the discussion moving, asking clarifying questions, and supporting students to think more deeply about the text. Now that we've explored ways to use student questions and observations to fuel classroom discussion, we'll next explore strategies for improving the quality of these discussions.

Improving the Quality of Discussion

When Chris first tried launching book clubs in his second-grade classroom, he quickly found that his students' attempts at discussion looked much more like organized turn-taking than an authentic, back-and-forth dialogue, as they went around the circle sharing their notes with the group, one-by-one. In doing so, they wound up talking *at* their classmates, instead of talking *with* them.

We shouldn't be surprised when we see these patterns of speech emerge because they reflect the shape of dialogue that has long been the norm in elementary classrooms – that is, students waiting patiently for their assigned turn to share something. Oftentimes, this is what students assume we expect of them. In the world of "sit silently and raise your hand", students aren't used to building real discussion in a classroom setting. Additionally, the few opportunities students *do* receive are often dominated by the teacher, where each child's contribution is directed toward the adult, rather than toward their peers. In doing this, we are teaching them to listen for the opportunity to speak, not for the opportunity to gain insight, to reflect, to ask more questions; in short, to engage in critical discussion. So, how do we support our students to have classroom discussions that mirror the patterns of talk they are *already* employing in other parts of their lives? To do this, we help our students establish new norms for classroom discussion and then scaffold them into building onto one another's thinking.

Establishing Norms for Classroom Discussion

Our first step is to draw upon the students' funds of knowledge regarding what authentic conversation and discussion looks like. To do so, we simply ask them to describe what talk looks like around the lunch table at school. To support their thinking, we can ask questions such as:

> If I were observing a conversation at the lunch table, what would I see happening? What does it look like? What does it sound like?
>
> How many people are often part of a lunch table conversation?
>
> How do people know when they can/should speak?
>
> Are there any unspoken expectations of one another?
>
> Do any problems ever arise? If so, how do you deal with them?
>
> How are these discussions similar to/different from our classroom discussions?
>
> Which style of discussion (lunchroom vs classroom) do you prefer? Why?
>
> How could we incorporate these lunchroom types of discussions into the classroom?

Next, we ask our students to establish a list of class norms – descriptions of what they expect to see and hear from one another. Depending on age, it might be best to do this as a whole group or to send kids out to brainstorm ideas in small groups before reporting back. Once the class has created their list of norms (see Figure 3.1 for an example of this from Rafa Navarro's fifth-grade classroom), we can have our students act as young researchers, showing them a video of children (or adults) engaged in a discussion and having them list the things they see the participants doing to make it so successful. These notes can then be compared against the class norms they previously created, adding any new

FIGURE 3.1

Student-created Norms in Rafa Navarro's Fifth Grade Classroom

Voices from the Classroom

Rafa Navarro

As a first-year teacher, I have received so much advice from others around me. The biggest, and what I feel is most important, is to build good relationships. I always encourage my students to share stories, facts, or tidbits about something we are learning. These daily conversations create opportunities for me to ask them more difficult questions. Oftentimes when I read a book or we learn something, my students will bring in a question or a comment about it the next day so we can talk about it. Making conversation a big part of our school day has helped with their understanding

– Rafa Navarro, fifth-grade teacher

items they feel are important. From our experiences doing this work with young children, we have found they often name things such as attentiveness, bodies facing one another, frequent eye contact, ability to largely stay on topic, and most everyone contributing. Students also notice the importance of participants building onto one another's ideas to build a cohesive discussion. Because building onto the ideas of their peers isn't evident in nearly enough classroom discussions, this is a skill we must explicitly teach.

Supporting Students to Build onto One Another's Thinking

One of the primary reasons we don't see students building onto the ideas of those around them is because teachers have traditionally taught students to take turns sharing ideas with the teacher at the front of the group, instead of with one another. We've all seen this countless times – the teacher gathers the class, asks a question, and then calls on students one-by-one, providing some sort of response to each child's contribution before calling on the next person. Even the positioning of the students' bodies, often sitting side-by-side and facing the teacher, plays a large role in ensuring the teacher is the focal point of discussion, not the class.

There are a few ways we can address this. The first is to incorporate more opportunities for students to circle up so that they can all see one another. You may find yourself having to say "Look at the class when you're speaking, not just me", but with time and a deliberate effort on your part to avoid speaking back to everything that is shared, students will begin talking with one another. This step is critical to helping them build on one another's ideas.

Another strategy is to provide lots of models for what these discussions should look like. As mentioned earlier, we can access videos of people engaged in discussion to identify the components of a quality discussion. However, when scaffolding them into the act of building onto the ideas of their classmates and teacher, we ask our students to pay careful attention to what this looks and sounds like. One great strategy is to have a fishbowl discussion where a small group of children sit in the middle of the class circle and have a discussion while the rest of the class watches, listens, and takes careful notes about what they notice about the connections that are made throughout the discussion.

For instance, you can ask four volunteers to create a small circle in the middle of the group to discuss issues they have with the quality of food offered in the school cafeteria (or any other topic that is likely to evoke a passionate discussion). Before the discussion begins, you will support the students in the larger circle who are conducting research by providing prompts such as

- How often does the group connect their thinking to something someone else has already said?
- What sort of language do they use when they are trying to connect to someone else's idea?
- In what ways do their connections make this a stronger discussion than if everyone just took turns saying things that were unrelated to one another?

Of course, because the students who have volunteered to be in the "fishbowl" know what their classmates are looking for, they will go out of their way to make all sorts of connections throughout their discussion. It's very likely you'll hear lots of them saying "Connecting to so-and-so, ..." because they'll want to make it very clear for everyone what they are doing. That's absolutely fine as it's a great way to begin. But with time, you'll be able to help them identify other stems that promote connections such as "Yeah, that's like...", "I agree with [insert name] because...", or "I disagree because..." (Hass, 2020). This last one, disagreement, requires some specific scaffolding as well.

Supporting Students to Challenge One Another's Thinking

The first step in helping students learn to value the role of disagreement is to normalize this practice for them. In theory, this shouldn't be too difficult given the fact they already disagree with others in their lives quite often. To draw upon this prior knowledge, launch a discussion where you ask students to name all the things they find themselves disagreeing about – with each other, with their families, with people within their various communities (neighborhoods, sports, church, etc). Once they've exhausted their examples, invite them into discussion by asking

> Why do you think you have disagreements about [name a particular issue]?
>
> Why doesn't everyone just think the same?
>
> Why do you think disagreements sometimes turn into arguments? How can we avoid this?
>
> How can we disagree with someone in a way that makes them more likely to listen to what we have to say?
>
> In what ways do disagreements sometimes help us understand something better?

Helping students make connections between disagreements in a class discussion and the disagreements they already have in so many other parts of their lives helps them begin viewing this as a natural part of discussion. Furthermore, inviting them to explore the reasons we disagree (different depths of knowledge as well as personal preferences, desires, goals, and life experiences) can later become a frame of analysis when critiquing beliefs that seem to be harmful to particular groups of people – for instance, "What might lead someone to believe a woman isn't as qualified as a man to be president?"

Next, acknowledge that you understand people sometimes feel uncomfortable in class when someone disagrees with something they've just said – despite the fact they hear disagreement from siblings, cousins, friends, and parents quite often. Ask them, "Why do you think disagreeing feels more comfortable in some parts of our lives – say, at home – than it does when we're sitting in a circle here in the classroom?" It might be helpful to provide students with a hypothetical example of a time when someone feels uncomfortable having people disagree with them.

Metacognitive discussions like this one are a major shift from what is the norm in so many classrooms where teachers simply tell students what to do and how to do it. In contrast to such an approach that positions students as passive receivers of information (Friere, 2000), we are strongly advocating for instructional practices that position children as primary meaning-makers who reflect upon their own experiences and practices in an effort to collaboratively create knowledge that will improve the quality of their individual and collective learning. Not only does this consistent reflection, analysis, and evaluation lead to better classroom practices, it positions our students to become more agentive. Consider this: which student is more likely to take civic action – one who is taught to sit silently and follow the rules others have made up for them or one who is a constant participant in analyzing the classroom as they work to democratically create agreed upon norms and practices?

Lastly, to scaffold our students into becoming more comfortable with disagreements in class, we need to launch many discussions that will elicit differing viewpoints and then invite them to reflect on how the discussion went and what role disagreement played in helping them understand the issue more fully. Kevin McArevey, a principal at Holy Cross Boys in Belfast, Northern Ireland, has developed questions that serve this purpose beautifully. Each week he has the students at his school go home to discuss debatable topics with their families such as:

> Is it okay to eat meat?
> Should you tell lies, or not?
> If you believe it to be true, is it?
> What is a hero?
> Should bullies be looked after the same as the victim?
> Should we be forced to donate our organs?

Extending Discussions into Our Students' Homes

Asked why he feels it is so important that his students engage in these discussions at home, Kevin McArevey explains, "I [want] to use children to educate adults through philosophical themes such as loneliness, anger, bullying and death. These issues are very important to our lives every day…[also] I am fighting against screen time and the digital age and want to bring back conversation, especially around their family table" (McParland, 2023). Because his students engage in similar discussions at school, having them extend this practice into their homes invites families to become an important part of the discussion; providing them an opportunity to hear about what is being explored in the classroom and to offer their own perspectives. To support families into success, Kevin suggests that they:

- Ask lots of questions
- Listen carefully to their child and avoid doing most of the talking
- Pose problems; play the devil's advocate
- Admit that they don't have all the answers

Similar to Kevin's practice of sending home weekly questions for students to discuss with their families, Chris created a special notebook for each child (dubbed their "Communication Journal") where students and their families had weekly written conversations (Burke et al., 1998) around thought provoking questions. A written conversation is just as it sounds, an exchange of ideas between two or more people that is written out on paper rather than discussed verbally. In addition to helping children develop stronger written communication skills, these artifacts of their thinking allow students to revisit what was discussed at home and share it with the class, as well as later revisit these conversations to see if their thinking had changed over time. Below, Meredith, a second grade student, has had a written conversation with her mother about whether or not zoos are ethical.

> MEREDITH: In our class we have been reading about zoos. Some articles said zoos are good for animals. Some articles said they are bad. What do you think and why?
>
> MOM: I have been goin to our zoo since I was a little girl. I used to go with my grandfather. I still love going with you! I think it is a really good zoo and I think the workers truly love animals. But a lot of times I think the animals don't look very happy. So, I guess I am not sure what to think?
>
> MEREDITH: I think zoos are good for animals because zoos are working harder than ever to save endangered animals around the world.

MOM: I agree – if they truly love animals and are working to keep them safe around the world, then I think they are working hard to keep them happy inside the zoos, too. I think having zoos also gives people jobs and creates a beautiful space in a town (instead of a mall) and makes people think about something other than themselves, too.

MEREDITH: But some zoos sell or trade baby gorillas. And other zoos have animals imprisoned in zoos. And one zoo got a police man to shoot a gorilla when he was escaping, and after that teenages threw rocks at the gorillas.

MOM: Yes. And those are really good reasons that zoos are bad. And that makes me very unhappy. But I think it's really hard (like, impossible) to do something that's 100% right. So I think you try your best and keep paying attention so you can fix your mistakes.

MEREDITH: So you are saying that no matter how bad of a thing they do you think the zoos will fix it?

MOM: No. I said I think you can always make mistakes or find a negative. Right now, with the facts you've presented, I think zoos are a good thing and doing their best to save the animals.

MEREDITH: Ok. So you are saying that when the zoos do a bad thing they will fix it.

MOM: I think if the worker truly love animals and are working to save animals, then they will do their best to fix mistakes and do better.

MEREDITH: Ok.

To prepare your kids for this work alongside their parents/caregivers, it would be helpful to first have them conduct a number of written conversations in the classroom with their peers. In fact, this is a wonderful way to have them think more deeply about titles from the critical text sets you develop to help them begin wrestling with important issues in their community. Furthermore, you can send these same texts home for the kids to read with their families and then invite them to share their thoughts with one another through written conversation. In the following exchange, Tatum, a third-grade student, and her mother have just read *Harlem's Little Blackbird: The Story of Florence Mills* (2012) as part of a class inquiry into community activism. While Tatum's mother begins with a few simple questions to gauge her daughter's understanding of the story, they later challenge one another to consider how this story can impact their own desires to create positive change.

MOM: Tatum, what did you like the most about this story?

TATUM: That people are very inspired by other people.

MOM: What do you think the theme of the story is?

TATUM: Don't judge a book by its cover.

MOM: What was the thing she always thought to herself?

TATUM: What else can my voice do?!

MOM: Do you think that you have to be a certain age for your voice to matter?

TATUM: No. That is a stereotype.

MOM: Do you remember how old Florence was when she realized the power of her voice?

TATUM: She was around six years old.

MOM: Other than her voice, what is Florence known for?

TATUM: Being the first Black singer (woman) to make history.

MOM: There's more. What is it?

TATUM: Help other folks.

MOM: I really liked how she used her gift to change other people's lives. How does her story impact your life?

TATUM: Help others and not just let them live on the streets. How does this impact your life?

MOM: I think I can find my voice using my talent. I am not a singer, so maybe my voice translates into being an advocate in healthcare.

As Tatum and her 21 classmates returned to the classroom to share their thinking about what it means to be an activist or to create positive

---

Voices from the Classroom

Tatum Williams

"We talked about these types of issues a lot in class – equal rights for all types of groups, equal pay, and other issues. We especially talked about how we can become better people and help the people around us. We were learning that even though we were young, we could make a difference. It helped to talk about this at home too because sometimes people could connect more with their families and feel safe sharing. My advice to teachers is to not feel afraid to talk about important issues with your students. It might be an uncomfortable space sometimes but this is something that needs to be done".

– Tatum (now reflecting on her experiences in elementary school)

change, they drew upon the understandings they developed alongside their family members. In doing so, an important connection was made between learning at school and learning in their homes.

Classroom Examples

To illustrate the power of creating space for children to engage in meaningful discussion, we offer two classroom examples. In the first vignette, second-grade teacher Rutland Martin follows his students' lead as they try to make sense of the relationship between a person's skin color and their ancestry. In the second vignette, fifth-grade teacher Tianna Myers creates space for her students to address a behavior issue that emerged in art class. In both examples, we see students playing an important role in guiding the discussion.

Second Graders Discuss the Potential Relationship Between Skin Color and Ancestry

During Morning Meeting, Rutland Martin asks his students if anyone has a question or an observation they've written in a classroom journal that they would like to share. Jordan raises her hand and reads something she's written in the Culture Journal.

JORDAN: I am one-quarter Black because my parents are white and my Granddad is Black.

After a short pause, a few other students begin to share connections to Jordan's statement before Michelle raises her hand to disagree with what she has heard.

MICHELLE: When I was a little girl, I thought a quarter Black wasn't a thing. Now that I'm grown up and I'm seven and I'm a big girl now I'm starting to think about the colors of our skin. Jordan, you're not a quarter Black but a mix of half Black and half white. If you have a Black parent or a grandparent, you're Black.

JORDAN: My mom and dad said that I'm a quarter Black because I'm white and Black so I got a mixture of skin.

MICHAEL: But your mom isn't Black, though. Her skin is kind of the same color as me.

JORDAN: She is half white and I'm a quarter Black. She does have lighter skin than me.

After providing his kids space to explore the relationship between skin color, ancestry, and race, Rutland steps in to clarify the reasoning being used to determine how Black or how white a person may be.

RUTLAND: It sounds like some of us are judging based on how light someone's skin is. Is that how you're understanding it? Does how dark or light we are tell us anything about our race?

MICHELLE: Well yeah, like how light a quarter Black is and how dark a quarter white is.

RUTLAND: You know, that's interesting because I used to think that way too. I remember a basketball player once who was Black, whose family was Black, but his skin was lighter than mine. For a time, I wasn't sure he was Black, but he was. So if we only go by how dark or light someone's skin is, maybe that's not the best way to decide what groups we might belong to, what race we are, or what cultures we claim as our own. What do you think?

MICHELLE: Yeah, and I'm not judging anyone. I'm just trying to tell facts about what is a quarter Black and what is a quarter white. What is mixed, what is Black, what is white.

JORDAN: It's just that my family is mixed. My mom's dad is Black so I'm one quarter Black.

MICHAEL: I just have one person in my family who is white and that's my aunt. She's the only one that is white so I try to not make her feel bad that she's the only one.

There are so many things to appreciate about this discussion. First, it was student generated. Jordan had had a discussion at home about her racial identity and was excited to share what she learned with the rest of the class. This discussion lays the groundwork for a continued discussion around race and skin color – one that could include important texts such as Lupita Nyong'o's (2019) *Sulwe*, a book about a young girl whose black skin is darker than the rest of her family's. Secondly, Michelle feels confident enough to disagree about the use of the term "one-quarter Black" (in a later discussion she clarifies that she doesn't believe there is such a thing as one-fourth Black because that implies you're not fully accepted as part of the Black community). At the same time, Jordan feels equally confident pushing back against Michelle's understanding of race because it doesn't match the important discussions she's already had about her racial identity with her family. In sharing this, Jordan pushes Michelle to consider another perspective.

And lastly, Rutland does a masterful job of creating space for the kids to take ownership of the discussion. The students are speaking to one another as he facilitates from the side. In this discussion, facilitation means being a listener and stepping in, as necessary, to clarify what's being shared and consider whether it might be an example of problematic thinking – assuming skin hues truly tell the story of a person's culture or race. Rutland uses himself as an example of faulty thinking in an attempt to diffuse any potentially hurt feelings.

Fifth Graders Address a Behavior Issue from Art

In this example, a student in Tianna Myers' fifth-grade class wants the class to talk about a behavior issue that emerged earlier in the day during their art class. Tianna is deliberate in using classroom discussion as a means of having her students analyze the development of their classroom community, both naming what is working well and thinking carefully about those things that need to be revisited or revised. One way she does this is to provide a Community Journal where students can record things they want the class to discuss.

LIAM: So I have the community journal. I just wanted to talk about what happened at the end of art today. A lot of people were yelling and they were just, like, out of control.

ISAIAH: Yeah, there were people at one table and while [the art teacher] was talking they were like joking around and laughing and playing while she was trying to teach.

JAYDEN: Yeah, connecting to Carsen, she would have to try to get everybody's attention multiple times. She would have to say, "Class, class" and use different things to get our attention.

GREG: I wasn't even able to get my painting done. I still had to do my trees and my people and I wasn't able to get started because I couldn't hear the instructions.

TEACHER: So does anyone who may have been part of the distraction want to speak to that?

SHAUN: That was my table but I disagree. I wasn't playing while she was talking. I was listening and trying to do the right thing.

TORI: I disagree with you because when she was teaching you and the person next to you were joking about your paintings. You were like, "Look at my painting!" and getting people to laugh.

MICHAEL: I was talking but I wasn't playing around.

ANTHONY: I disagree. You and other people got up from your table and walked over to one another to talk and you guys were really loud.

IZZY: Yeah, I was loud when I was talking and I also was talking with people at other tables. I'm sorry.

CAMERON: I was too. I was going over to other tables and like talking and playing around during the lesson. So, I'm sorry for that.

CHLOE: I'm sorry that I was talking and playing around when she was trying to teach.

SHAUN: I'm sorry that I was talking too.

TEACHER: Thank you for that. Another important part of understanding this is to recognize the consequence for talking and playing around. What happens when we act this way?

GREG: Some people may be unable to learn or to get their work done.

TEACHER: Right, that's what is most important. I appreciate everyone at that table for taking accountability. The problem isn't that you can't talk. It's that you can't talk over others and you have to respect the space. Was there anything else?

AMARI: People were also not talking very good about their paintings and that's really not healthy. I ask that we don't do that.

TEACHER: That's a good point. I know I'm guilty of doing that sometimes, too. Like saying, "This is so bad. I'm not very good at this". That doesn't help us learn. Thanks for reminding us of that, Amari.

AALIYAH: We need to be confident in ourselves.

CAMERON: Yeah, I think I was just a little upset about my painting because it didn't turn out how I was reasonably planning for it to turn out. Because when I first looked at how it was turning out I was like, "Am I really supposed to be doing that?" It was just kind of…

LAILA: I'm pretty hard on myself, too. And [the art teacher] has helped me with that a lot.

Do you all remember that butterfly video we watched earlier in the year? How many times it took that boy to revise his sketch until he got it the way he wanted it? Just never give up. Don't talk down on yourself. You have to always lift yourself up.

In this discussion, we hear these children reflecting on issues from earlier in the day while working democratically to build expectations for one another as a learning community. Students demonstrate courage and vulnerability when speaking honestly about their experiences as well as their own role – whether it be playing around or talking negatively about themselves as artists. This is a wonderful example of how classroom discussion can take many different forms and serve many purposes – all while teaching students how open dialogue is an important part of meeting the needs of our communities. In the next chapter, we will explore how to engage students in research around important issues.

CHAPTER 4
Helping Students Conduct Research

Once while working with a school in West Virginia, Lester spoke at an evening event for families. When the evening concluded Lester signed books and chatted with folks and then headed to his car. He put his things away in the trunk, got in the car, and lowered the top. He noticed a young boy watching intently from the entrance to the school. Lester smiled and waved, and the little boy came running up with his mom close behind. "How did you do that? How did you make the ceiling go down?" the boy asked. "Stand right here (next to the driver's door) and I'll show you". Lester touched the toggle switch that controls the convertible top. "Watch. When I push that switch forward the top goes up", Lester said as he raised the top. "Now what do you think I have to do to make it go back down?" The boy beamed. "Do you pull it back the other way?" Lester smiled. "If you would like to find out you can reach in and pull that switch back". The boy gently pulled the switch, and his eyes widened as the 'ceiling' folded down behind the seats. "That's like magic", he said.

Magic, indeed. There is magic in the natural curiosity of children. Children want to know; they seek information, they question, they try out things. They marvel and delight in new discoveries. That inquisitive attitude is the headwaters of research. Research can begin with something as simple as an observation that leads to wondering and generates a question that drives us to know more. As educators, we can create situations that introduce students to new ideas and experiences that ignite wonder and questions. We can lead them to resources where they can explore perspectives and seek answers to those questions. Through their research, we can teach them to seek out multiple resources, accumulate information, compare, synthesize, think critically, and refine their questions to continue with further inquiry.

In this chapter, we detail what this type of complex, joyful research can look like in the classroom. But first, let's consider how this relates to student's development as young agents of change. To set our students up for success as researchers and activists, we must take into consideration the need for culturally relevant research, learning that is rooted in the needs of the community, and the ability to become critical consumers of information.

Engaging in Culturally Relevant Research

We are all cultural beings. We are shaped by our beliefs, our values, and our experiences. Using a culturally relevant approach to engage students in the research process connects learning to their home lives, their lived experiences, and their prior knowledge (Gonzalez et al., 2005; Ladson-Billings, 1995). At times, culturally relevant research provides students with opportunities to explore their interests. At other times, this work focuses on challenges and issues within their community, connecting learning to the real world. When we center students' lives, and their ways of being, and connect to issues within their communities, they will likely be more motivated and enhance their self-perception as capable and knowledgeable researchers.

What Does This Mean for Our Teaching?

When developing opportunities for our students to engage in research, we need to be certain that the opportunities grow out of our students' lives, inside and outside the classroom, as well as from the interdisciplinary content we are tasked with teaching. Of course, this is easier to do when there are many opportunities to conduct research throughout the school year – some confined by specific content (i.e. the Upper Mattaponi Tribe), some growing purely out of student interest (i.e. teach us about something you love), and other research that accomplishes both at the same time (i.e. a country that has particular significance to your family). Some of this research will be small inquiries that will last only a day or two; while others will demand weeks of reading and writing to explore in depth. Providing opportunities that vary in depth, time, and autonomy is key to helping students become engaged as researchers.

For example, at the Center for Inquiry in Columbia, South Carolina, teachers and administrators take a school-wide approach to determining what research needs to look like across their students' experiences in k-5 classrooms. Each grade level incorporates two "expert projects" into their school year. These expert projects are multi-week research projects that end with a Share Fair, a public presentation of their work in the school's large hall where classes take turns coming out for twenty minutes while the children in the host class teach them from research boards, posters, self-created books, slides, and more. Over the course of each year, and across the whole of their elementary school experience, they conduct projects that are connected to both the curriculum and their lives and interests. While some of these projects change year-to-year, Table 4.1 shares what some of these projects have looked like over time.

TABLE 4.1

Sample Expert Projects at the Center for Inquiry Across K-5 Classrooms

Kindergarten	**Expert Project 1:** Passion Project For these very first expert projects, students create a tri-fold board or poster that shares five facts about something they love and want others to know more about. These include all sorts of engaging and personally relevant choices like crystals, soccer, high heels, baking, garbage trucks, chess, puppies, and Barbies. **Expert Project 2:** Endangered Animals In support of their study of animals, students choose an endangered animal to research and teach others about.
First Grade	**Expert Project 1:** Grandparent Project As part of their inquiry into "Life Long Ago", students select a grandparent or elder to interview and then use all that they learn to create a book about them that includes both text and photographs. Among other things, their research focuses on family stories, traditions, inventions, and descriptions of transportation, homes, clothing, and schools. **Expert Project 2:** Author Study Students select a favorite author and research their lives, writing process, and books. Their final projects include a presentation board that shares all they learned about their author as well as a child-created book that is written in that author's style.

(Continued)

TABLE 4.1 (Continued)

Second Grade	**Expert Project 1:** Animal Adaptations While studying about animal classifications and adaptations, students select an animal they would like to learn more about. This research provides them opportunities to learn about their animal's habitats, diet, and physical and behavioral adaptations. This information is shared on a poster using headers and subheaders to organize their information. **Expert Project 2:** Country Research As part of a global learning unit, students research a country that has particular significance for their family. Many students choose to write about the countries their families have immigrated from (either recently or long ago) while others choose places they have been or would like to visit.
Third Grade	**Expert Project 1:** Biographies In response to research they have already conducted to find out how seldom the histories of women and people of Color are included in the mandated social studies textbook, students select someone from one of these marginalized social groups to research. They use their research to write a biography that is added to the classroom library. **Expert Project 2:** Changemakers After spending much of the year keeping up with current events and discussing issues that face their classroom, school, and local communities, students select one issue to research further. These often include topics like homelessness, litter, stray animals, deforestation, etc. Part of their research focuses on ways others have taken action to address this issue.

TABLE 4.1 (Continued)

Fourth Grade	**Expert Project 1:** Astronomy Articles As part of their astronomy unit in science, students select a single aspect of astronomy to research while also conducting a genre study of scientific articles in their writing workshop. Once their research is complete, they write articles of their own teaching others all they have learned. **Expert Project 2:** Historical Figures For this interdisciplinary project, students research a historical figure that fits within their social studies unit of study and then craft a historical fiction story sharing key pieces of what they learned.
Fifth Grade	**Expert Project 1:** Ecosystems While researching specific ecosystems, students identify the food chains and food webs that are found there. Students then describe the relationships between various elements within the ecosystem, constructing a diorama that features each of the components of the food chains and food webs and how they are interrelated. **Expert Project 2:** Impact Project Students select an issue in the community they want to better understand. With components that include text-based research, interviews, and connections with local experts and organizations, this research stretches over the course of the entire year and calls on students to use all they have learned about research over the past 6 years to create projects that have a positive impact on their community.

Connecting Research to the Needs of the Community

People have been actively involved in identifying issues and engaging in research to improve their communities for centuries. For example, Black literate societies created in the 1800s served as a vehicle for collaborative research to develop knowledge, advocate for rights, and fight injustice (Muhammad, 2020). The shared knowledge cultivated in Black literate societies empowered them to fight racism and seek liberation. In Indigenous communities, oral histories, storytelling, and art are common methods used to share knowledge and seek solutions. For example, Indigenous people communicate traditional knowledge about land use and environmental stewardship to protect sacred land and inform conservation efforts. Similarly, urban planners in large cities conduct community-based research by involving residents in the planning process to ensure their needs and concerns are addressed when developing land, building roads, repairing bridges, adding traffic lights, etc. When research is conducted in conjunction with real issues that affect the community, there will be greater involvement and a higher potential for meaningful change to occur.

What Does This Mean for Our Teaching?

While our students will conduct many types of research throughout the year, we must ensure that some of these opportunities call on them to dig deeper into community-based issues that have emerged from their reading or during discussions in the morning meeting. For instance, after a read-aloud leads to a discussion about bullying or food insecurity, we might ask, "If we wanted to change this, what more do we need to know? What questions do you have?" The ensuing research could be a whole class effort or be conducted by a single student whose job it is to look up information and report out. Either way, students learn that research is a key aspect of better understanding the issues within our communities so that any action they may take is more likely to be well informed.

Let's explore what this looks like in action. In preparation for the biography project described in Table 4.1, third-grade students at the Center for Inquiry conducted research to see how often, and to what depth, the contributions of women and people of Color were included in their social studies textbook. One group of students researched the names provided in the textbook's index to produce a tally of how many of them represented historically underrepresented social groups, as opposed to white males. Others went through the textbook and tallied who was shown in the photographs and illustrations. The final group collected notes on the placement of information about underrepresented groups. Not surprisingly, when the class brought all their data together they found that the vast majority of historical accounts were about white men and that any information about other groups (particularly those who were Indigenous, black, Latinx, or female) was often restricted to just a few isolated chapters, placed in a few call out boxes as an aside, or briefly mentioned in the final page or two of the chapter.

This research helped the class more fully understand the need for texts that teach about the important contributions made by those from marginalized social groups. The class then conducted a second round of quick research to identify historical figures from underrepresented social groups whose contributions were not included in the social studies textbook. These names became the focus of the research they conducted when learning about, and creating their own, biographies.

Voices from the Classroom

Abby Bowen (now reflecting back on third grade)

"I think it is important for everyone to make positive changes in the world. A lot of people do not and don't want to, either. The projects we did [in elementary school] really opened up my perspective on what has happened and what is happening in the world and its importance".

Becoming Critical Consumers of Information

As situated products of the world, texts transmit cultural and political messages (Mirra, 2018). Whether consuming printed information within the pages of a book or journal, or from print, visual, and/or audio on the screen (TV, computer, phone, etc.), we must remain critical and read against the text (Kelly et al., 2023). Reading against the text involves understanding that each text is presented from a particular perspective and that other perspectives likely exist. It also involves an awareness of the fact that some perspectives represent those with power and may deliberately exclude other perspectives. Reading against the text, then, includes challenging limited viewpoints, and seeking more information to gain a better understanding. In this way, we acknowledge that no text is neutral. We question the author's ideologies, intentions, and beliefs. As readers, then, we ask questions such as:

- What is the author's background and expertise?
- Is the author credible?
- What does the author want us to believe?
- How does the author benefit from this work?
- Who else benefits?
- Whose perspectives or voices are excluded?

If our students are to become critical consumers of information it is necessary to build background knowledge essential to the construction of informed opinions, to develop expertise, and to establish credibility. To explore any topic in depth, it is important to gather, compare, and critique information from multiple sources (read/view the news from different outlets, talk to neighbors and friends with varying opinions, etc.). This includes seeking the perspectives of those who have been historically marginalized. We have a responsibility as critical consumers of information to disrupt the status quo that typically ignores the voices of those who are harmed to maintain and perpetuate a system of inequities.

What Does This Mean for Our Teaching?

When students begin the process of reading and notetaking, they are not likely to recognize that an answer from a device is not a comprehensive look into the topic and does not lead to a grounded understanding. Finding a quick answer in isolation may provide a sense of knowing without developing background information or conceptual understanding. Therefore, student researchers need to access a wide variety of texts while learning to read with a critical eye. Reading critically positions us to compare information, examine various perspectives on a topic, and determine whether information is being intentionally slanted in one direction. When students find information that contradicts or seems off, they should pause and ask:

- Who is presenting this information?
- How is it different from other sources?
- What information has been added or is missing?
- What are the publication dates of each source?
- What perspective is being favored or fronted here?
- What perspective is being ignored or excluded?
- What other sources can I find to compare this information?
- How do I present this information?

As a reader you know that you have the right to question a resource and you often do. Our students must also feel comfortable pushing back and reading against the text to raise questions regarding perspective and bias. As student researchers, they will need guidance with knowing how to share their findings in ways that recognize that various perspectives exist on almost every topic.

For example, when teaching about bias, Chris invited his second-grade students to an inquiry into zoos. To frame this study, he posed the following question, "Are zoos good or bad for animals?" Over the course of two weeks, the class read a wide variety of texts about zoos that included picture books, news articles, opinion pieces, websites, and a novel. These second-grade researchers quickly found that each author (say, someone from an animal rights group versus someone writing in support of zoos) very selectively chose which pieces of information to share and how they would shape this information for readers. For instance, those arguing against zoos were less likely to mention the work zoos do in support of endangered species while those in support of zoos were less likely to describe the mental and physical toll of animal imprisonment. Throughout the study, the students kept asking themselves questions such as those posed above as they came to understand one's perspective, as well as one's purpose for writing, plays a significant role in determining what gets shared and how that information is communicated to readers.

Not Sure Where to Begin? Try This ...

When supporting students to engage in research that can lead to action, one of our primary goals is to help them develop the critical thinking skills necessary for such work. In this section, we detail what this can look like in the classroom as we teach students to carefully tune in to their natural sense of curiosity, build expert vocabulary, develop broad questions to shape the research, locate relevant resources, and collect needed information.

Research Begins with Curiosity: Moving from Story to Questions

One way to launch research is to use a fact-infused story to pique student interest and trigger a flood of questions that can fuel an investigation of an issue, problem, or topic. To begin, curate a collection of texts that includes one or two fact-infused fiction picture books and ten to fifteen nonfiction texts focused on various aspects of the topic (see Table 4.2 for a text set about the creation of laws, how they can negatively affect marginalized groups of people, and how people have taken action to change them). Introduce the topic with the fiction selection. In this example, we begin with Pittman and Mercer's (2020) *There Oughta Be a Law*, a fictional account of two children visiting the State Capitol to learn how a bill becomes a law (Table 4.2).

Read the selected text aloud without stopping to question, lift vocabulary, turn-and-talk, or offer connections. Just read it all the way through to allow the students an opportunity to listen with purpose and gain an overview of the text. When you reach the end, ask the students to sit with the story for a moment and think about new words they heard, information that surprised them, information that made them wonder, and/or information they didn't understand. Give them a couple of minutes to reflect and jot ideas. Then ask them to read through their

TABLE 4.2

Samples from Curated Text Set for Research About Rules and Laws

Fact-Infused Fiction Texts	Nonfiction Texts
There Ought to Be a Law by Portia Pittman & Calvin Mercer *Lillian's Right to Vote* by Jonah Winter	**Government/Creation of Laws:** *Understanding How Laws are Made* by Matt Bowers *How the Government Works* by Syl Sobel *Know Your Rights!: A Modern Kid's Guide to the American Constitution* by Laura Barcella *State Government* by Karen Kenney Video: Schoolhouse Rock, "I'm Just a Bill" **Effects of Unjust Laws on People/Change Makers:** *When the Schools Shut Down: A Young Girl's Story of Virginia's Lost Generation and the Brown V. Board of Education of Topeka Decision* by Tamara Pizzoli *How Women Won the Vote: Alice Paul, Lucy Burns, and Their Big Idea* by Susan Campbell Bartoletti *Until Someone Listens: A Story About Borders, Family, and One Girl's Mission* by Estela Juarez and Lissettte Norman *The Case for Loving: The Fight for Interracial Marriage* by Selina Alko *Malala's Magic Pencil* by Malala Yousafzai *Good Night Stories for Rebel Girls: 100 Tales of Extraordinary Women* by Elena Favilli and Francesca Cavallo

notes and put a star next to three things they most want to ask about. Provide three small index cards and ask them to write one question on each card, but do not add their name. Once they've finished, collect the cards and read each question aloud, asking the students to help you decide whether the question is:

- clarifying meaning of a word (Vocabulary)
- asking for a fact or small bit of information (Facts/Information)
- seeking to understand a big idea or develop a concept (Concepts)

When the questions are sorted, take note of what has captured their interest, what has made them wonder, and what has perplexed them. Doing so allows student inquiry to drive our instructional decisions, including text selection and focus. For example, if you find that most questions are asking about the meaning of words, you will likely select a less complex text focused on introducing and extending vocabulary as a follow-up read-aloud. In the example above, there is a diversity of texts, both in content and complexity, that explain how governments work to create laws. Likewise, if a cluster of questions asks for a bit of information to clarify a misunderstanding you may offer a follow-up text with a tighter focus that targets the specific information in question (Laminack, 2019, https://therobbreviewblog.com/uncategorized/read-aloud-lets-flip-it/).

The follow-up read-aloud experiences featuring nonfiction from the curated collection demonstrate how text resources can be intentionally selected to target our questions. Delving into a few of the nonfiction resources will layer new vocabulary and new information which will give rise to new questions. Pause at times to reflect and note how questions become more refined as we gain new vocabulary, new information, and deeper understandings that help us develop a broader conceptual frame for the information. For instance, after learning about how laws are made, texts that demonstrate the effects of unjust laws on everyday people will likely lead students to ask increasingly rich and pointed questions about equity and injustice. After engaging with each resource, pause to ask:

- What new vocabulary have we learned?
- Which of our questions can we answer now?
- What new questions have emerged?
- What can we ask now that we couldn't/didn't ask before?

After you have read aloud several of the follow-up texts, return to the question cards and remove those that can now be answered by the group. Ask students to jot the answers on the back of the card and then return them to the set before reading aloud and sorting any new questions generated from the nonfiction read-aloud experiences.

Clustering Questions to Identify Categories

Next, gather the class and examine each of the three stacks of questions (vocabulary, facts, concepts). Ask them to help you cluster the questions by categories/topics as you read each question aloud. Sorting questions by topic or category helps students recognize the relationship between and among vocabulary and ideas within the topic. This process also helps demonstrate how information is often organized within nonfiction resources.

As students begin to cluster questions and name the clusters, point out the connections between these and headings, listings in a table of contents, and index entries in nonfiction books. Select a few of the nonfiction resources to demonstrate how the use of text features such as the index, the table of contents, or the glossary will help students narrow their search and stay on topic when working within their research groups. Then ask students to select a heading for one cluster of questions (see Table 4.3). Use the table of contents, headings, and index to find segments of text presenting information that will contribute to answering one or more of the questions in that cluster. Demonstrate that

TABLE 4.3
Clusters of Facts with Headers

Creation of Laws	Lawmakers	Voting	Injustice	Change
Where do ideas come from for laws?	Do they have to take a test or go to school to be able to make laws?	How do they get votes if they make bad laws?	Why would people make laws to keep people from voting?	Why don't they change the bad laws right away?
Can regular people (voters) make laws?	Do they have other jobs too?	Do voters know about all the laws?	Did the United States have laws against women going to school too?	Can people not in government change laws?
How long does it take?	Who gets to be a senator?	Why can't kids vote too?		Can kids change laws?
How do they make laws about stuff they don't even understand?	Why aren't there more women and Black people making the laws?	Do other countries do it this way too?	Why do racist people get to make laws? Why don't they fire them?	Do people get in trouble for trying to change a law?
Why don't people get to vote on laws?	How much do they get paid?	How does someone get to be a candidate? Does it cost money to be a candidate?	What other laws are bad?	

using these tools will lead them to specific texts, and sections of text, that will assist in gathering the information they need for the question or category they are researching. Student researchers can be overwhelmed by the density and volume of resources. Learning how to use text features to narrow the search and discovering that one does not always need to read the entire text can reduce that anxiety and make their work more efficient.

Building Expert Vocabulary

Involving students in sorting and clustering questions will require a good deal of conversation and scaffolding. While students work together to formulate and refine questions about the topic, this is a great opportunity to point out the importance of developing content-specific vocabulary. You can help them recognize that communication without access to a shared expert vocabulary results in less efficient conversation and research. Take the time necessary to co-construct a core shared vocabulary before jumping into the resources for reading and note-taking. Explain that as researchers who will want to speak and write about their work with a sense of authority and expertise, they will need to build a vocabulary specific to their topic.

Start with brainstorming expert vocabulary, a list of words they believe an expert would need to speak and write about the topic effectively. For the example we've created here, we can expect words such as candidate, legislator, democracy, bill, law, justice, oppression, repeal, and so forth. As students offer words, record them on a chart and ask them to explain what the word means and why it will be important to their work as researchers and as advocates. This will provide insight into the scope of their initial understandings. When they have exhausted their known vocabulary, return to the nonfiction collection and select a less complex title focused on developing vocabulary for the topic. Use this opportunity to demonstrate how even a simple book can help us expand our vocabulary.

Before you begin reading, tell students your intent with this read-aloud is to expand the list of expert vocabulary. Their task is to notice specific words that would help them read, speak, and write about the topic. As you read aloud, pause at times and invite students to add words to the list. Again, as they offer new words ask them to explain why the word should be included, and what they think it means. At the end of this read-aloud take stock of the expanded list and note how reading one book added to the vocabulary. Of course, this list will continue to expand as students begin delving into the resources for their research. Repeat this step with a second book if you feel it is necessary for the core vocabulary.

TABLE 4.4

Expert Vocabulary Sorted into Clusters

Creation of Laws	Government	Voting	Injustice	Change
Democracy	Government	Representative Democracy	Justice	Repeal
Bill	Constitution	Election	Civil Rights	Activist
Law	Lawmaker	Candidate	Oppression	Advocacy
Veto	Republican	Campaign		Lobby/Lobbyist
	Democrat	Polling		
	Legislative Branch	Political Party		
	Executive Branch	Electors		
	Judicial Branch	Electoral College		

Review the expanded list and guide students to organize the expert vocabulary into clusters. They may find it helpful to review the cluster headings from the question chart since the vocabulary may fall into similar clusters. As with the questions, clustering the expert vocabulary nudges students to search for connections between and among words, to see and name categories, and to begin thinking conceptually about the topic. See Table 4.4 for an example of what this might look like.

Developing Broad Questions to Guide Research

Developing an expert vocabulary leads to more specific and efficient conversations about the topic as students begin to rethink and refine their questions. Return to the vocabulary clusters and talk about why those words belong together. Next, invite students to use their expert vocabulary to generate broad, big idea questions that can guide their investigation of print and digital resources.

In the beginning, students may have a difficult time distinguishing between a broad question and smaller, fact-based questions. These smaller questions are ones that can quickly be answered by a simple online search. For instance,

> How old do you need to be to be in congress?
> How many legislators vote on a law?
> What happens if there is a tie?

TABLE 4.5
Developing Broad Questions

Small, Fact-Based Questions	Broad Question
Can people not in government change laws? Can kids change laws? Do people get in trouble for trying to change a law?	What rights and responsibilities do citizens have when it comes to creating and repealing laws?

On the other hand, broad questions are ones that are a bit more conceptual and demand that we dig deeper. Oftentimes, a few smaller questions coming from the same category can be woven together to develop a broad question. For instance, as Table 4.5 demonstrates, three questions from our Change cluster can be combined to shape a broader question speaking to the role we can all play in creating change.

This new question would call on student researchers to study, among other things, multiple forms of advocacy and activism that people have engaged in to educate and persuade legislators. The purpose of developing broad questions such as this one is to provide the needed shape and purpose for the research. Using this broad question as a guide, the focus shifts from simply gathering isolated facts one might see on a social studies quiz to seeking out nuanced answers to questions that are essential to a given topic or issue. Of course, they will still seek out answers to these smaller questions but now can they see the relationship between these individual pieces of information and how they can be stitched together to answer bigger, more pressing questions.

Locating Relevant Resources

Learning how to locate specific information within a collection requires student researchers to tap their expert vocabulary as they review each resource for its potential to provide information relevant to their guiding question. This initial perusal of resources will be more efficient if students learn to make use of text features such as the table of contents and the index.

Start by inviting students to select the broad question they are most interested in and use this interest to form research groups. When your groups are formed, bring out the curated collection of resources. These may include physical books as well as digital resources. However, the initial work will be limited to the resources in the collection you have curated. The focus for the first visit with the resources is learning to use expert vocabulary and selected text features (e.g. table of contents, index, glossary) to appraise each resource for its potential to provide information pertinent to the group's guiding question. This is not a time when students will be reading and notetaking, although they will find all sorts of intriguing information and want to jump right in. The focus at this time is previewing and sorting the titles within the curated collection to determine which ones will be most useful for each group.

This initial sorting of resources is an important step in learning to stay focused on the work at hand, the research question. We all know how tempting an interesting, and perhaps unrelated, bit of information can be like quicksand that rapidly sucks you in, consumes all your time, and pulls you hopelessly off task. Students will be just as easily distracted by images, catchy headings, and infographics that capture their attention and derail their focus. Therefore, the focus at this moment is checking the table of contents, the glossary, and the index to determine whether the title contains information pertinent to your question.

When student researchers begin the work of finding relevant resources, offer each group a few sticky notes to list titles that are to be added to the group's collection. It will be easier to keep track if each group has a dedicated color sticky note. Of course, some titles, especially the more complex ones, will be on the list for several groups. This process will help young researchers narrow the set of resources to a smaller number that will be more manageable and more focused when they begin the process of reading and notetaking.

The interest generated from read-aloud experiences, developing expert vocabulary, and crafting, sorting, and categorizing questions will result in a buzz as students delve into the collection of resources for the first time. And because everyone has been engaged in all phases of the work, each group will be aware of the guiding questions of every other group. So, you can expect that there will be lots of resource swapping and students from one group announcing they have found a great resource for another group.

This first foray into exploring resources with the goal of weeding out those that will not contribute to your search can be confusing. In the process of reviewing a source for its relevance to their research question, students will inevitably get sidetracked by something interesting, but off topic. It is important to end each research period with a quick whole-class check-in to debrief. This not only provides a forum for students to share findings and resources, but it also provides an opportunity for the teacher to highlight the process and help students learn to remain focused.

Creating a Graphic Organizer to Focus the Research

The next step for young researchers is to organize their questions and begin the process of reading and notetaking with their selected resources. For some students, this can feel a bit overwhelming. Offering an organizing frame will make this step more accessible and manageable. One option is to use mind maps to organize and cluster their questions. The topic or category is written in the center and surrounded by questions that are clustered by topic. The central, big idea question for each topic is surrounded by smaller questions that can be the focus of specific research to build a broader understanding. As you can see, the work we did earlier in collaboratively grouping the students' questions and crafting broad questions from these is key here.

While the broad questions are necessary for locating resources, smaller related questions fuel the research within those resources. This leads to the need for crafting more specific smaller questions in service to the big idea question. The challenge here is a focus. Students are great at popcorning questions, but ensuring the questions are focused and related to the central question guiding their research is more challenging. The mind maps (see Figure 4.1) are a useful

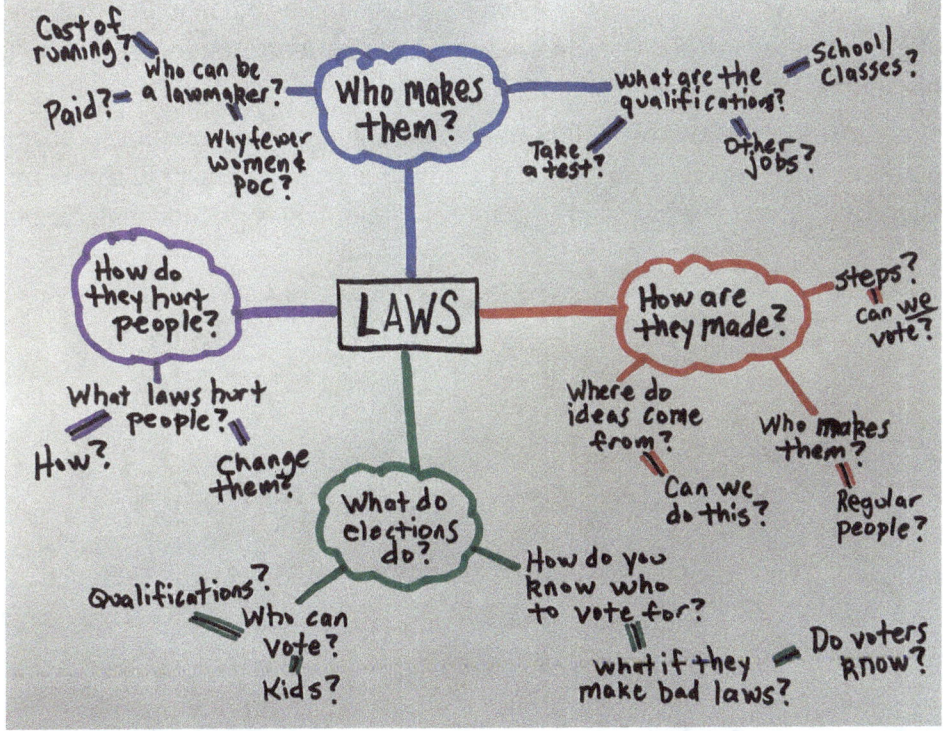

FIGURE 4.1

Mindmap Organizing Questions Related to Laws

tool because they provide a visual representation of spontaneous thinking which can, upon review, be checked to ensure all bits are related to the whole (Figure 4.1).

Classroom Example

To illustrate this process in action, we share an example from a third-grade classroom. In this example, students in Lisa Helsel's class are engaged in a research project focused on honeybees. As the students learn more and more about this topic, their research eventually leads them to identify actions they, and others, can take to be better stewards of the earth.

The project began with a read-aloud of *The King of Bees* (2018), a fact-infused fiction picture book, and continued with a carefully selected collection of nonfiction texts, physical books and digital texts, focused on honeybees. Their research was launched by questions generated from the fiction read aloud which sparked interest in the topic and a robust discussion.

That initial discussion gave rise to the need for developing a topic-specific "expert" vocabulary that students needed to speak and write more precisely about the topic. Lisa selected one of the less complex nonfiction texts to read aloud and invited the students to take note of expert vocabulary that they organized into categories on an anchor chart. Students continued adding to this chart across the project (Figure 4.2).

As students developed their expert vocabulary, their questions became more specific as well. Lisa and the students clustered their questions and developed a broader "big idea" question for each cluster. Students indicated

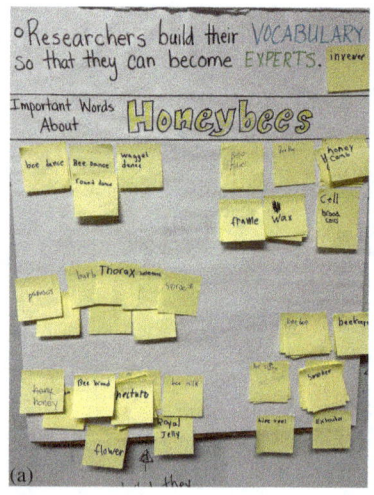
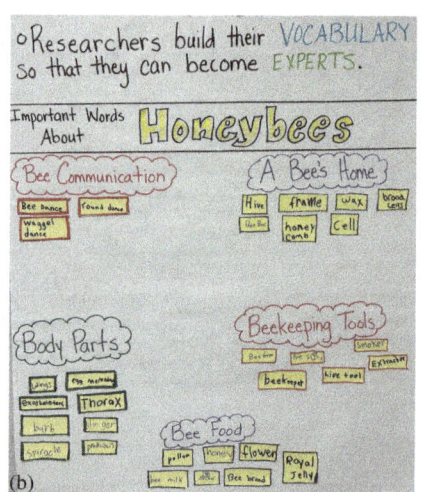

FIGURE 4.2(a, b)

Expert Vocabulary Chart

which big idea question most interested them, and Lisa formed research groups around those interests.

To begin their work, each group spent time with the collection of nonfiction resources checking the index and table of contents to create a list of resources relevant to their big idea question. With the collection of resources narrowed down to a manageable set, each group began the work of reading and notetaking. Lisa showed the students how to use mind maps, and a graphic organizer, to organize their big idea questions and cluster smaller, more specific questions that would help them locate facts and bits of information they would need to synthesize as they worked to address the big idea questions (Figure 4.3).

Each group member selected one question from their group's mind map to guide their reading and note-taking. To facilitate the note-taking process and to help students develop an understanding of citing their sources, Lisa made a set of slides for students' Chromebooks. The students entered each small/specific question from their mind maps into the prepared slide where notes were added as they read. To introduce citing sources, Lisa showed students how to copy a photo of the source and paste it into the slide where they made notes from that source.

The more they read and gathered information, the more fascinated they became with honeybees. New vocabulary and new information positioned them to reflect on their new insights and refine their questions. Each day their debriefing meeting brought some new bit of information to the surface that helped each group see how their research was only a small piece of a larger project. Participating in the research process did more than fill their notetaking slides with information, they became intensely interested in honeybees.

Voices from the Classroom

Lisa Helsel, third grade teacher

"For many years, I controlled research topics, resources used, questions asked, and expected outcomes during our research writing units. Students developed note-taking skills, organized information into paragraphs, and revised their work, but the end result was often cookie-cutter versions of the same paper. Giving more ownership to students has resulted in a classroom of engaged researchers who use a process that mimics the work of people tackling real-world problems. It teaches students to be curious, critical consumers of information who know that the research process always leads to more questions. Relinquishing more control to students can be frightening, but, when teachers put trust in their students as writers, the benefits far exceed what students can do within the tight confines of a strictly controlled research process".

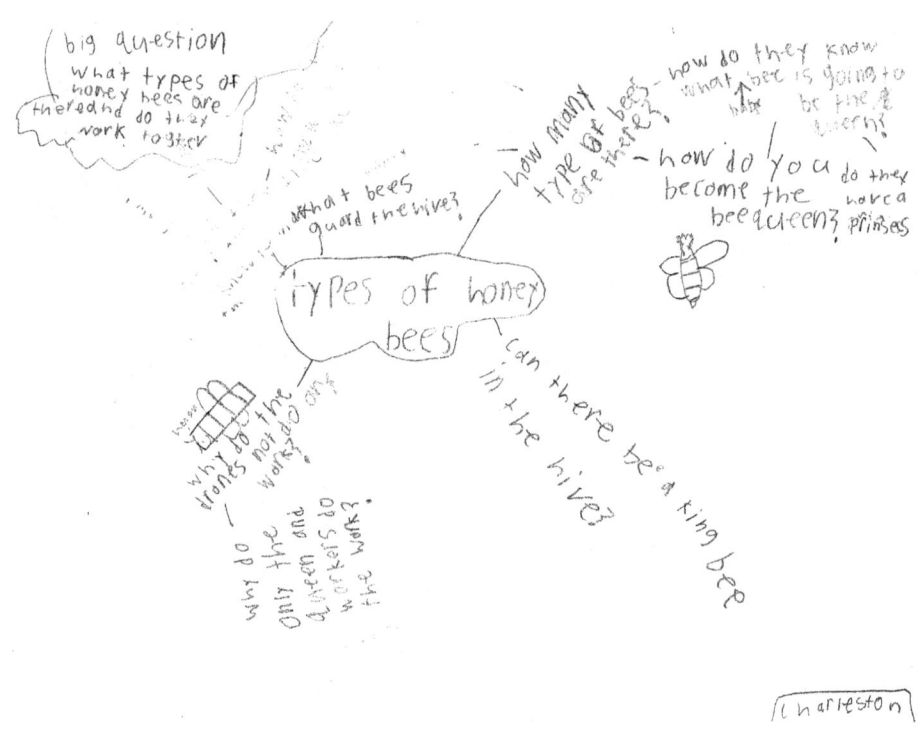

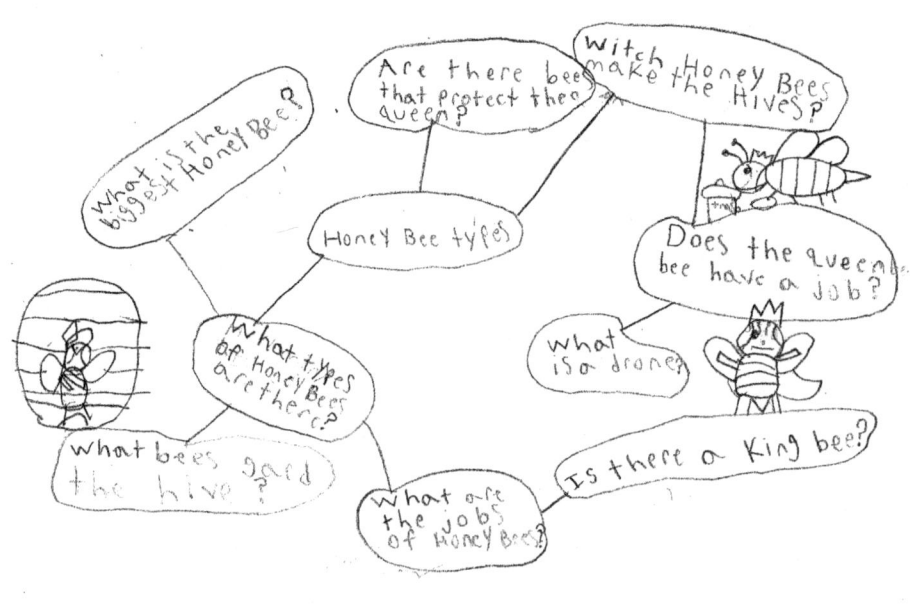

FIGURE 4.3

(1–18) Mind Maps

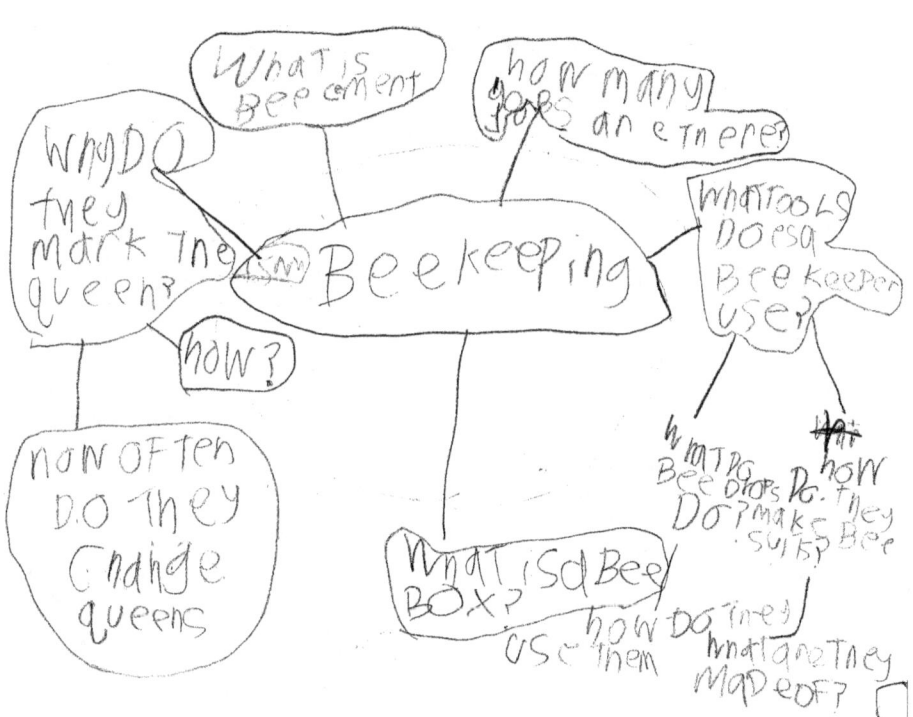

FIGURE 4.3 (Continued)

FIGURE 4.3 (Continued)

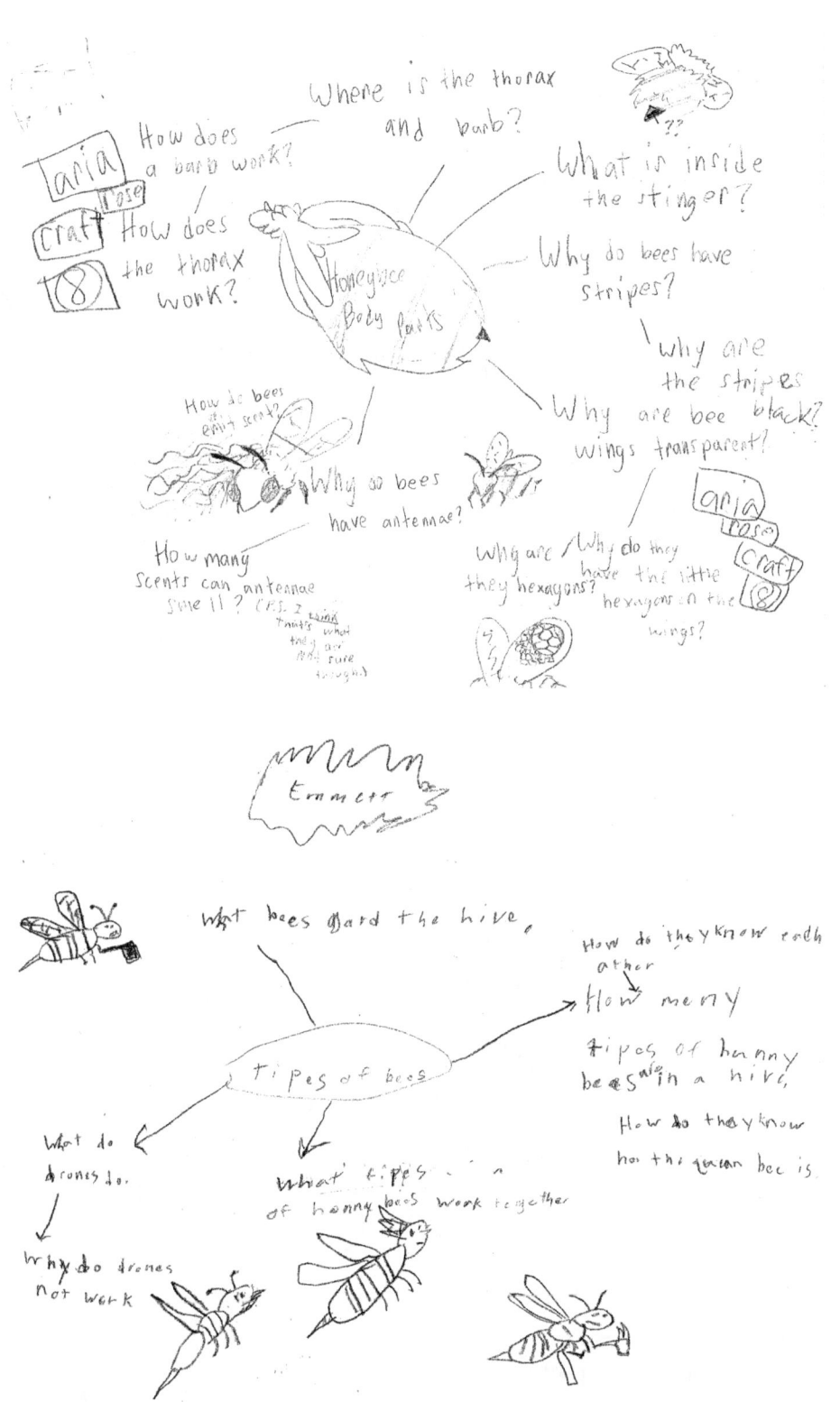

FIGURE 4.3 (Continued)

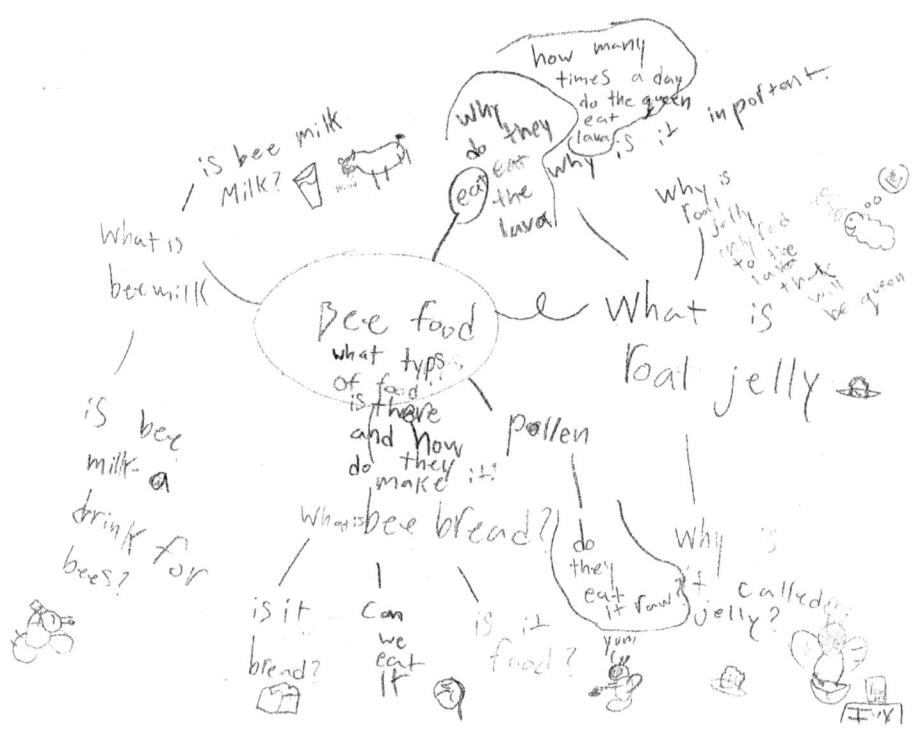

FIGURE 4.3 (Continued)

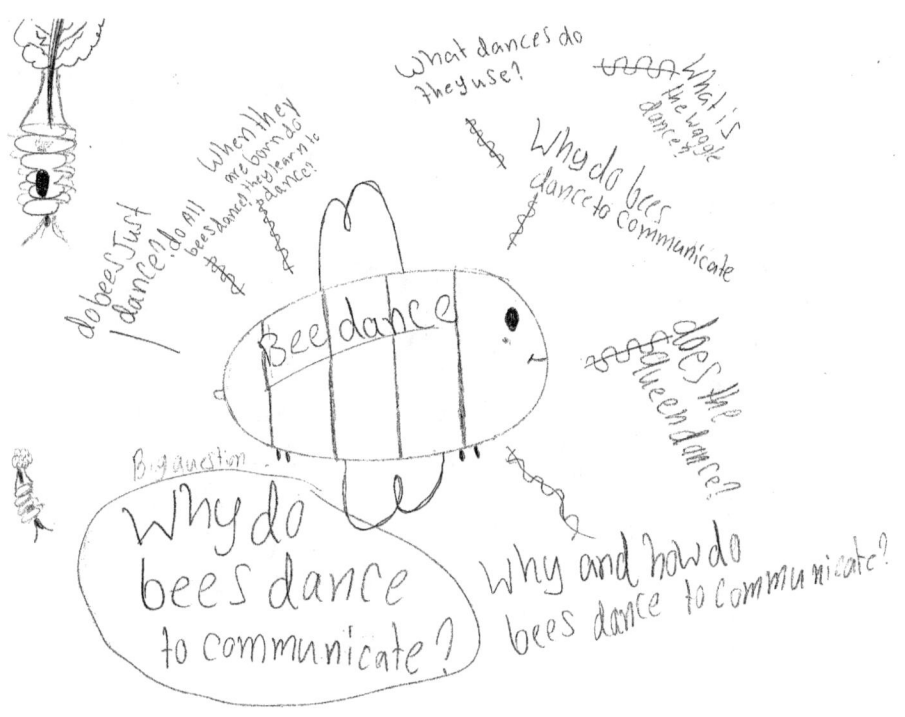

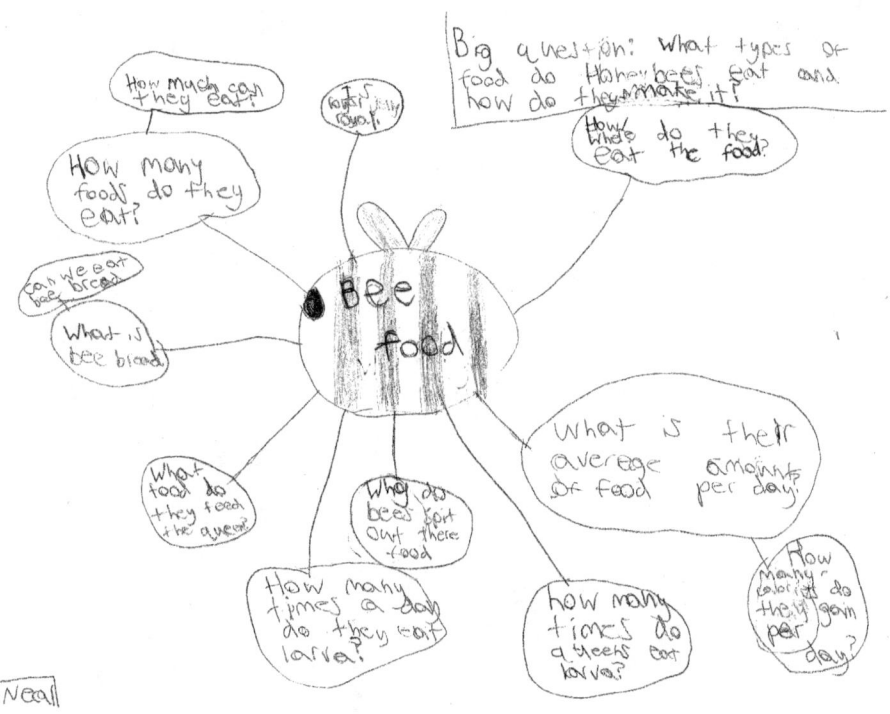

FIGURE 4.3 (Continued)

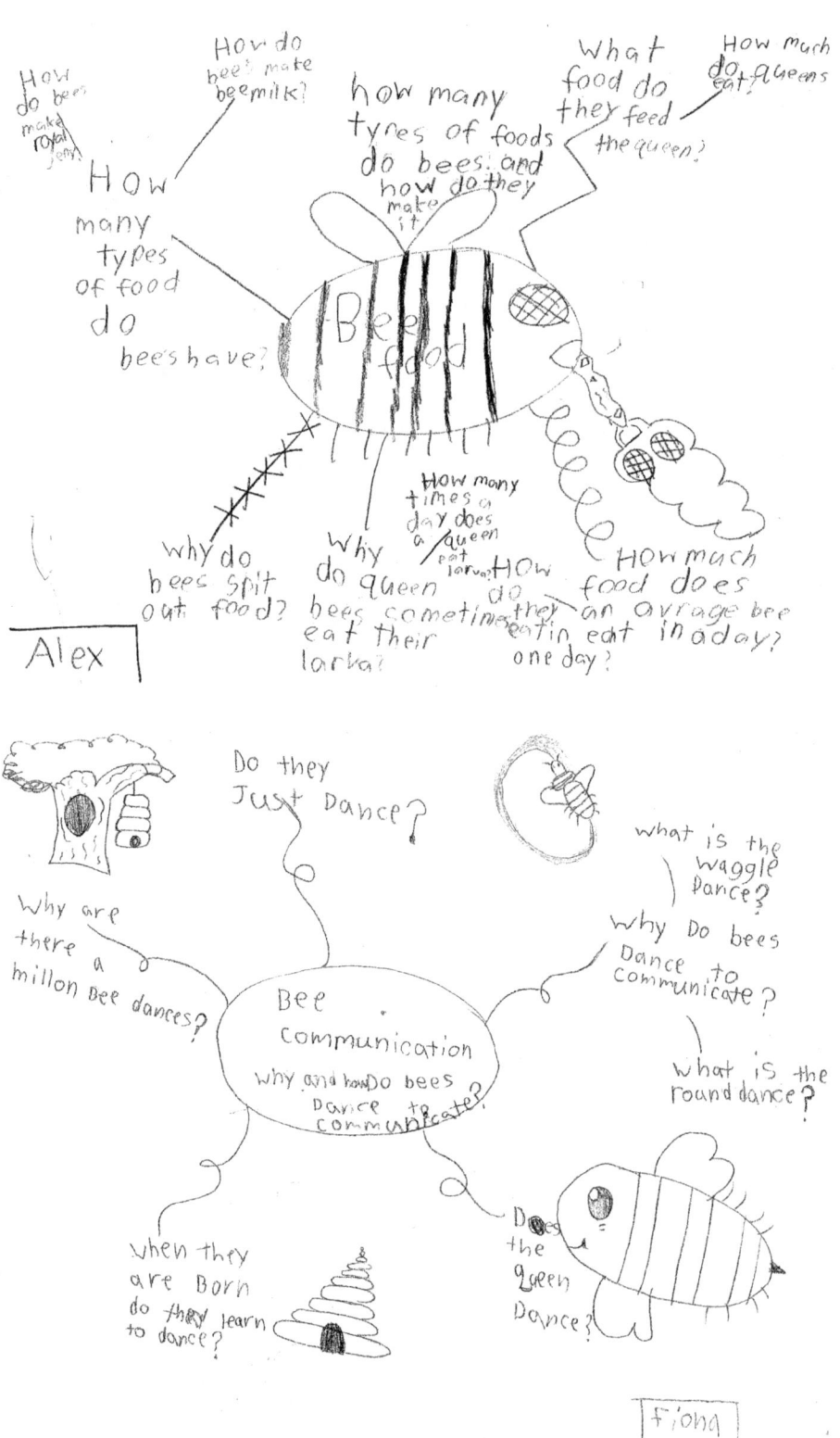

FIGURE 4.3 (Continued)

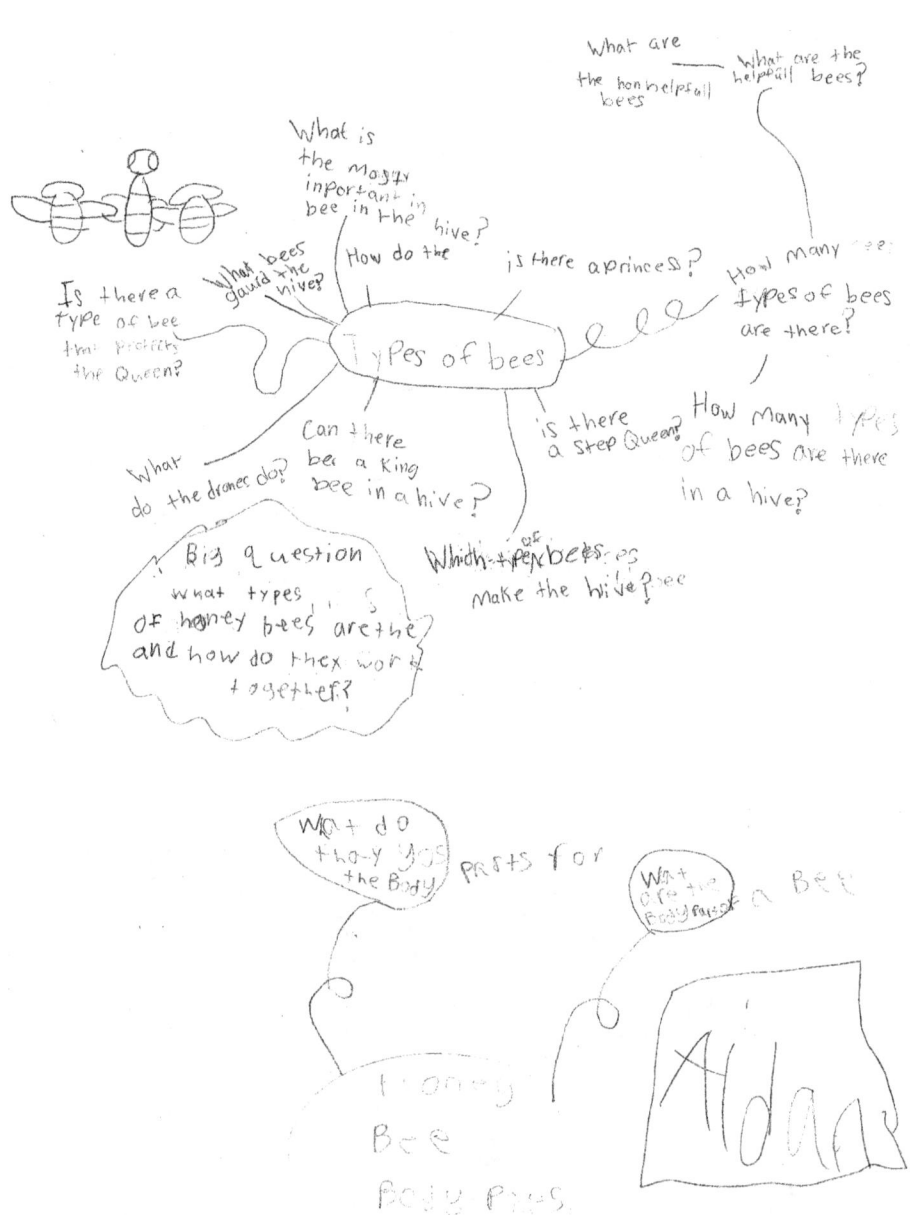

FIGURE 4.3 (Continued)

FIGURE 4.3 (Continued)

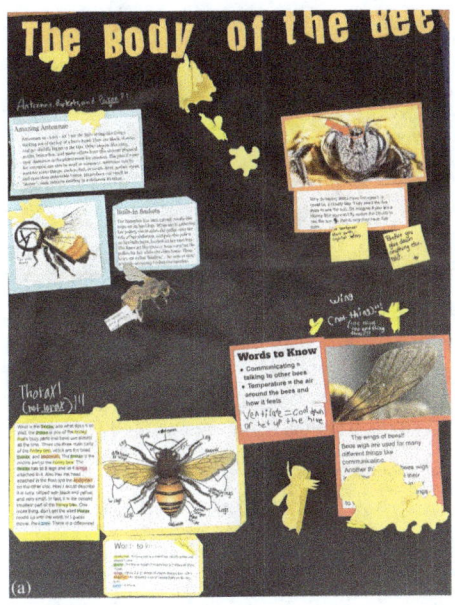 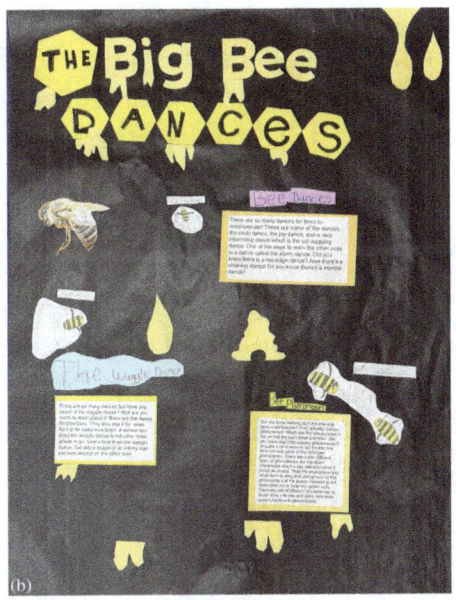

FIGURE 4.4(a, b)
Giant Book

As groups completed their research, they created an enlarged book page to share their findings. Each group decided what information to share and how best to present it. They studied their nonfiction resources as mentor texts to select specific text features that best matched their information and their intentions for sharing it (Figure 4.4).

Seeing all the giant book pages together gave each group a more comprehensive understanding of honeybees. That also gave rise to new questions and brought to surface a growing concern for the welfare of honeybees that led to a whole class discussion of the problems that bees face and their impact on the environment. Their research revealed that the main challenges faced by honeybees were created by humans. They created a list: habitat loss, fewer farms, larger farms growing crops that don't help honeybees, the use of pesticides and herbicides, climate change, and more.

As students continued to add to the list and discuss the impact of humans as a threat to honeybees one student recalled a detail she had read:

STUDENT: I think it was like, 1947 maybe, but something like 60% of the honeybees died.

LISA: That's an important fact and we will need to find the resource where you read that because when we start trying to persuade people as advocates in the next few days, adding those shocking facts is a great way to grab your reader.

This exchange presented an opportunity to revisit resources and read critically. Lisa reminded the student of the need to record information and its source for reference. She also noted that if that bit of information can be verified it would contribute to the argument that humans have a responsibility to help save bees.

Providing an opportunity for students to share findings that concerned them will often lead to a sense of urgency. The whole group discussion of problems honeybees face sparked a renewed interest among the students in Lisa's class. These third graders were adamant about the need to make people aware of ways they can help bees and stop being part of the problem. Lisa told the students that they could be advocates for honeybees and suggested that each of them choose one of the problems to address as an advocate. Then she explained that being an advocate means finding a forum where you attempt to persuade people to come to the aid of the bees.

LISA: You've worked in small groups, and we've talked about solutions to some of the problems bees face and I asked you, is there anything that excites you, that you'd like to do something about, teach somebody else about?

STUDENT: I chose, protect swarms because when people see swarms, they want to get rid of them and take down their hive.

LISA: Did you know there is a book called Bee Rescue, and it is about someone whose job is to go move swarms of bees from places they are not supposed to be. That would be a great thing for you to research and educate other people on.

STUDENT: We wanted to do two different categories, but we want to combine those. I wanted to give information on how to build a bee hotel and she wanted to tell how to plant diverse flowers for bees. So, we decided to put those together with No Mow May all in one infographic and have diverse flowers around the bee hotel and don't mow in May so the flowers will bloom, and the bees can live in the bee hotel.

STUDENT: I want to tell why pesticides are bad for bees and suggest ways to help without using pesticides.

STUDENT: I want to tell people to plant more meadows, forests, and urban green spaces.

STUDENT: I want to do loss of habitat because there are a lot of reasons for that. I could give suggestions to help.

The third-grade researchers created infographics and/or short videos to inform others about the threats humans pose and the role we play in the declining bee population (Figure 4.5).

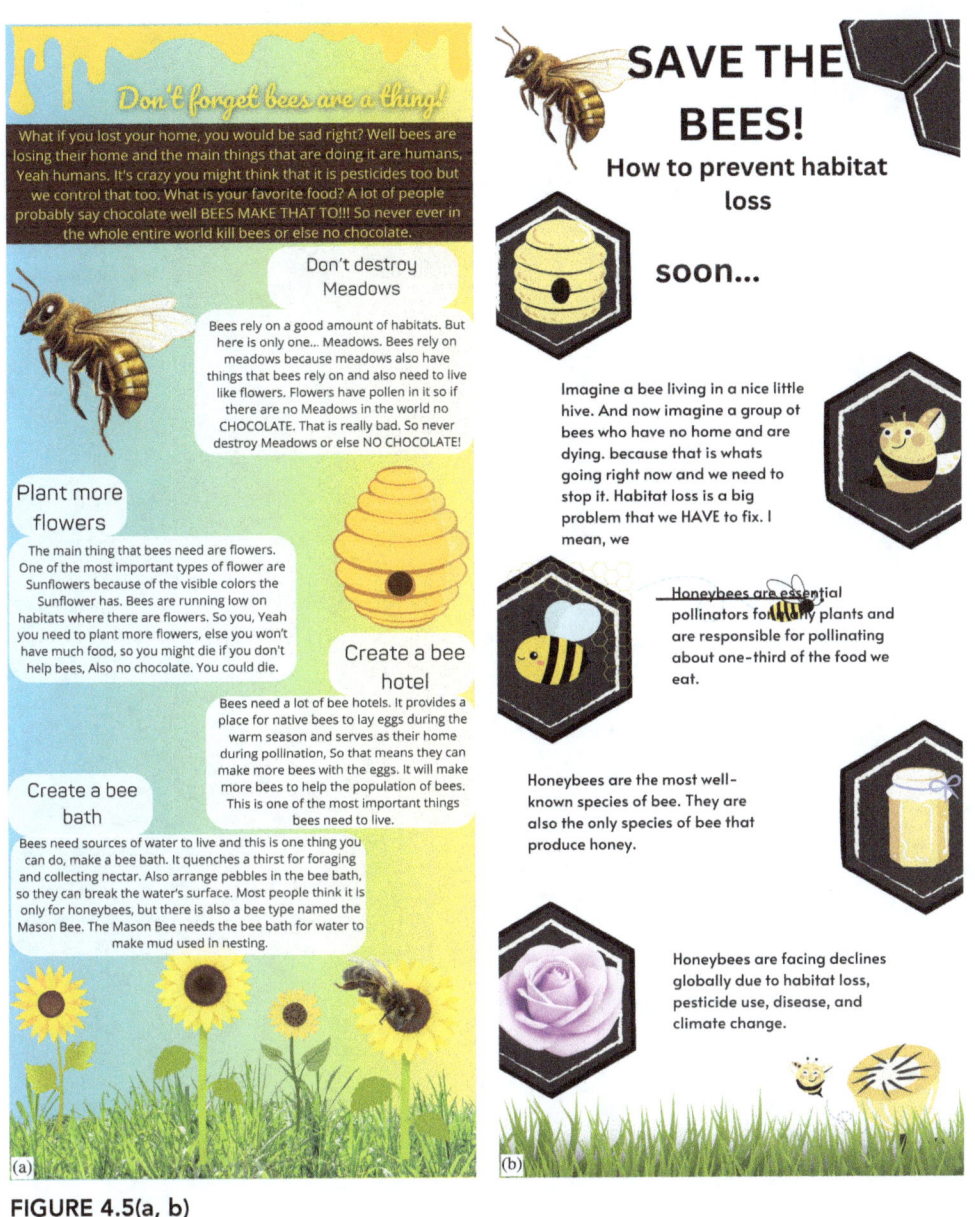

FIGURE 4.5(a, b)
Student-created Infographic

When research builds on the natural curiosity of children it expands their vocabulary, their questions, their insights, and their awareness of broader issues and concerns. New understanding often leaves students with a need to do something, to act, and help others become aware. That sense of knowledge as power is common in children. Perhaps if we help them learn appropriate ways to become involved in making a change, they will become the kind of adults for whom civic engagement is a way of being.

CHAPTER 5
Helping Students Take Action

One night in January, as he was busy preparing dinner, Chris received a text from a classroom parent. It read: *Ethan asked if he could write a letter addressed to all SC senators instead of reading tonight. I must say, it's pretty damn good.* Intrigued, Chris clicked on the attached photo to read Ethan's letter.

> Dear South Carolina Senators,
>
> I am a 3rd grade future voter. I'd like to discuss bill S419. Students like me deserve the right to learn more and test less. We want to have the opportunity to choose our own journey in school and select our own careers in life. My teacher and others deserve more funding, higher pay, and respect.
>
> Bill S419 prevents us from having all of the above and that is why I am writing this letter. Vote No! to Bill S419.
>
> Truly yours,
> Ethan [name retracted]

In the weeks leading up to Ethan crafting this letter, Chris had shared pieces of his own advocacy work to protect public education. This involved working with other teacher activists to share information about key legislation, support teachers to contact elected officials, cultivate a social media presence for educators, and organize rallies and demonstrations. Chris also invited his students to provide feedback on the bill Ethan would later write about – particularly those sections dealing with increased standardized tests and the retention of third-grade students based on a single test score. In addition to these classroom conversations, Ethan's mother, who was also a teacher, spent many car rides to and from school helping him understand her own concerns with the bill.

Equipped with multiple copies of his letter and a stack of envelopes, Ethan came into the classroom the morning after his mother's text and said he needed to use his school laptop to look up addresses for each state senator.

FIGURE 5.1

Third Grader Ethan Mails His Letter to Members of the State Senate

Over the coming days, a handful of his classmates began to trickle in before the bell to help him. Together, these eight- and nine-year-old advocates for public education prepared forty-six envelopes for delivery. By the end of the week, Ethan's letters were dropped off at the post office and his advocacy work had come to a close. Or, so it seemed (Figure 5.1).

A few weeks later there was a call for educators to show up at the State House as a show of force as Bill S419 was being debated on the Senate floor. Ethan and his mother joined Chris after school to watch the proceedings. After about fifteen minutes in the gallery, Ethan decided to return downstairs and request face-to-face meetings. Each senator Ethan pulled into the lobby was urged to vote no on Bill S419 and then handed a second copy of his original letter. One was so impressed that he brought Ethan's letter back to the Senate floor, stepped to the lectern, and read Ethan's words into the official proceedings. Soon after, a colleague from across the aisle stood to question whether Ethan's concerns had any credibility. Drawing on the frustration some were feeling with the efforts of classroom teachers to stop this legislation, he argued, "How can a third grade child know anything about this? I bet his mother is a teacher and he's just parroting what she told him". The skepticism Ethan received was even reported by the AP on social media. Not deterred, Ethan returned to class the next morning and proudly shared his experiences with his classmates, including the rebuke from the man he now referred to as "Senator Ugly Suit".

There are so many things we can learn from Ethan's journey into political activism. First, Ethan's work reminds us that we need to stop underestimating early childhood and elementary-aged students. For too long, education has worked from the false assumption that young students just aren't old enough, smart enough, or capable enough to understand and act upon the issues that face their communities. As many examples from across the globe show us (see Table 5.1), this couldn't be further from the truth. When given ample support and a vision for what is possible, students will rise to the occasion.

TABLE 5.1
Students Taking Action

Felix Finkbeiner, 9, founded an organization called Plant the Planet, which has helped to plant millions of trees worldwide. Plant the Planet now employs more than 100 people and has provided training to tens of thousands of children across 73 nations.	 https://www.cnn.com/videos/tv/2022/11/08/felix-finkbeiner-plant-for-the-planet-trees-spc-intl.cnn
Haaziq Kazi, 9, started a multi-year design of a device capable of removing large amounts of plastic trash from the ocean. Two years later he gave a TED talk in New York City and has since created the ERVIS Foundation to educate fellow children about the effects of mass plastic consumption.	 https://www.youtube.com/watch?v=fuK5rwfTxCQ

(*Continued*)

TABLE 5.1 (Continued)

Marley Dias, 10, used social media to launch the #1000BlackGirlBooks campaign, aimed at collecting a thousand books featuring Black female leads to donate to schools. In the 8 years since its inception, Ms. Dias has spoken at national conferences, hosted a Netflix show amplifying Black voices, authored a book, and collected more than 13,000 texts to be donated to schools.	 https://www.marleydias.com/
Greta Thunberg, 15, began skipping school on Fridays to camp outside Parliament with a sign that read "School Strike for Climate". Her actions inspired thousands of students around the globe to join her in a campaign that came to be known as "Fridays for Future". In the years since she has become a national voice speaking about climate change, in addition to other important issues.	 https://www.youtube.com/watch?v=tdDasG3ruRU

Secondly, Ethan's efforts remind us that student attempts at advocacy and activism will reflect their current understanding and academic capabilities. This should be readily accepted as an integral part of the process. Yes, Ethan's letter would have been more powerful had he pulled specific passages from the proposed bill, provided a more developed analysis, and shared his personal experiences as both a student and the child of a classroom teacher. As such, Ethan's letter served as a rich data point to inform Chris' future plans for a whole-class study of persuasive writing. Yet, just as we don't force toddlers to wait until they're able to correctly pronounce every syllable before stringing together a series of words, we mustn't wait until our students "get it right" before advocating for change.

Lastly, Ethan's efforts to stop this piece of legislation show us that public schools have the capacity to play an integral role in helping our youngest citizens become civically engaged – even when this means venturing into politically divisive topics. The conversations Ethan had in class about advocacy and current events helped him engage in richer discussions with his mother as she shared her own concerns, wishes, and plans for action. In this way, a true home–school partnership was forged; one that supported Ethan to make sense of the legislative process and the role citizens play in shaping their community's future. Had Ethan asked to write a letter supporting the bill, Chris' response would have been the same. Our goal is not to convince children to believe exactly as we believe or to support the same causes we champion. Rather, the goal is to help students take notice of what is going on in the world around them, question those things that don't feel right, access reliable resources to find out more, and move from talk to action.

Moving from Talk to Action

Up to this point, we've detailed the importance of helping students begin to take notice of the issues within their communities, develop a greater sense of empathy for the experiences and needs of those around us, engage in critical discussions alongside a diversity of peers, and develop research skills to deepen their understanding of complex issues. These are incredibly important learning goals that help create a more informed and compassionate citizenry. However, as classroom examples throughout each chapter of this book have demonstrated, we mustn't stop here. What good is it to learn about and critique acts of injustice, inequity, oppression, and environmental harm if we're not prepared to dismantle them? Without scaffolding our students into action, we send the message that becoming an armchair critic is enough – a belief that leads far too many adults to engage in virtue signaling on social media platforms without any demonstrable effort to create actual change within the communities they work, live, and play.

Why is this? Why are so many people willing to make public declarations of their supposed beliefs but far less willing to take actionable steps toward creating the change they want to see in the world? While there are numerous reasons for this, we're going to focus on three of the most common and discuss what these mean for our teaching.

Reason #1: "I Would Love to Do Something…But I Don't Know Where to Begin".

Many people feel as though they would love to get involved but are unsure what this would look like. A common response is to donate money to established organizations doing good work – the Equal Justice Initiative, the Environmental Defense Fund, and the Human Rights Campaign Foundation, to name just a few. Certainly, providing resources to advocacy groups that already have the infrastructure and expertise to create positive outcomes is a powerful use of one's time and money. However, action should not end with the sharing of a credit card number. When money becomes tight, giving is often one of the first items in the budget to be reduced, if not altogether eliminated. Furthermore, there are many issues facing our communities that require people to show up, speak out, and take a stand.

What Does This Mean for Our Teaching?

Our task is to help our students better understand what options are available to them as advocates for change. As will be detailed later in this chapter, we must explicitly teach students about the various forms advocacy can take and then provide them opportunities to put these into action in their own lives. Such a study could take shape as a formal inquiry stretched out over multiple weeks or could emerge in response to opportunities for activism as they arise.

Here's an example of helping students see options. Leah, a third-grade student in Chris' classroom, told him about conversations she'd been having at home with her mother, a school librarian. Leah learned that libraries across the district were severely underfunded and that many of the books in their collections were both outdated and non-representative of the student populations they served. Leah wanted to do something about this but wasn't sure what that might look like. Chris began by asking a few questions: (1) What would you like to see happen?, (2) What else do you need to know about this and where could we find that information?, and (3) Who has the greatest power to change this and how can we convince them to act?

Leah told Chris she wanted libraries to receive better funding so they could buy books that were more relevant to the lives and identities of students. Leah's concerns grew not only out of the conversations she'd been having with her mother at home but also from the many discussions she had in class focusing on the underrepresentation of marginalized communities in historical texts and trade books. After some thought, Leah and Chris decided she needed to conduct research to learn how much money school librarians received for their collections each year, where this money came from, and whether or not it was the same for every school. They decided interviewing their school librarian would provide her with the answers she sought, in addition to information her mother had already shared with her at home. Leah learned that while each school works independently to supplement monies for the library, the amount received from the district office was actually very little. This caused inequities from school to school. For instance, at Leah's school, the librarian could only afford to buy a couple dozen new books each year. Leah also learned the superintendent and school board had the power to make budgetary decisions and that a great way to call for change would be to deliver a formal request during the open forum at a future school board meeting.

Leah worked to take all she had learned and craft it into a speech that reflected her concerns as well as a formal request for more money (see Figure 5.3). A few weeks later, she showed up at the school board meeting with her family and when her name was called she stepped up to the microphone and called on the superintendent and school board to better fund school libraries across the district. As should be the case, she was well-received, thanks to the sincerity of her concern, the depth of her knowledge, and the merit of her demands. In collaboration with similar efforts being made by others within the district, the school board eventually approved a one-time general fund budget allocation of $25 per student to be used to update library collections. Helping connect Leah's concerns to concrete actions she could take was key in helping her develop the knowledge and agency one needs to become an agent for change.

Voices from the Classroom

Leah Johnson (reflecting on her experience in third grade)

"I was nervous when I spoke to the school board because I was, like, really shy and I didn't know what to expect. I think most of them listened but a couple of them maybe didn't because I was younger then and maybe they thought I didn't know much. I think it's important for kids to learn to do that though because as you get older you get more opportunities and you need to have those skills for what's to come".

Leah's Speech to the School Board

My name is Leah and I'm a third grader in [this district]. My mom is a middle school librarian. She loves that she gets to read books to kids and help them find books they like to read. I like to read too. I like animal books. Right now I'm reading Diary of an Ice Princess: Snow Place Like Home.

> This summer my mom and I read a book together called We Are Grateful. Unlike many books, this book was about Native Americans and what the Cherokees do during the seasons. It's pretty hard to find many books about Native Americans in the school library. It's also hard to find many books about other groups of people because those books are newer and not in our libraries enough.
>
> Something that worries me is that it's hard for libraries in the district to buy many books because they don't have much money. I interviewed our school librarian and she told me she gets $500 a year to buy books. A book costs her about $16.99. This means she only has enough money to buy 29 new books a year and we have 264 kids in our school. Because these hard books are so expensive, she usually has to buy the soft books and they get destroyed a lot.
>
> I would like if people would donate money to schools or for the district to spend more money on books. We like technology but we LOVE books. Thank you.

Reason #2: "I Would Love to Do Something…But I'm Only One Person".

It's common for people to feel overwhelmed by the enormity of the problems facing their communities, whether it be climate change, homelessness, or harmful pieces of legislation that appear certain to be adopted. Feeling they have no ability to create meaningful change alone, most people choose to do nothing at all. The year Ethan wrote his letter and then met with legislators at the State House, there were more than 60,000 public school teachers in the state of South Carolina who could have taken action alongside him. Yet, according to data collected by a grassroots organization of teachers in the state, only a few hundred educators contacted their elected officials to lobby against Bill S419. Imagine the impact, had legislative offices been overwhelmed with letters, calls, emails, and personal visits from tens of thousands of classroom teachers. There is power in numbers – but only when we first make ourselves accountable as individuals.

What Does This Mean for Our Teaching?

To support their individual growth, we must first help students learn to successfully collaborate with their peers. This includes supporting them to develop the skills necessary to navigate the challenges of collaboration as well as learning to use the ideas they hear to push their own thinking. As developing advocates and activists, collaborative efforts help provide students the support they need to confidently act on their own in the future.

In Nozsa Kyler's second-grade classroom, for example, students worked together collaboratively to analyze the dress code. In her class, students are routinely challenged to identify and critique the ways our society works to oppress marginalized populations of people. In addition to building space within their morning meeting for students to share their observations about the world around them and the occasional concerns that grow out of these, the class also engages in focused studies of African American Language and the cultural significance of hair. Included within each of these inquiries are opportunities to learn how the dominant culture has historically used differences in language and appearance to marginalize members of the Black community.

So as an extension of this work, Nozsa decided to have her class conduct a critical analysis of the school district's dress code. Knowing there were many parents, teachers, and students upset with the ways it unfairly targeted females and students of Color, this study would provide an opportunity for Nozsa's second graders to tackle inequities within their immediate schooling context. Over the course of two weeks, Nozsa and her students used part of their morning meeting time to read sections of the dress code together while creating a class chart detailing what they noticed, what they disagreed with, and what they struggled to understand. They also brought these discussions home so family members could offer their own perspectives. Drawing on stories they heard from older siblings, many students were upset by the fact girls were being held responsible for the unwelcomed attention of boys.

Voices from the Classroom

Nozsa Kyler, second- and third-grade teacher

"After learning all we could about the dress code, we decided to invite someone from the school district into the classroom so we could share our concerns. We also wanted to let them know what we wanted to happen. I was proud of my kids for asking the hard questions and not backing down when the responses didn't sound right to them. The kids learned that while we might not always get the results we want, we can continue to voice our concerns. They need to know it is our right and responsibility to notice things that don't feel fair and to stand up for what we want for ourselves and the people around us".

Many were also offended by the fact the district banned the display of hair picks, heavy jewelry, and do-rags – items many families in the classroom proudly used at home. To gain a broader context of this issue, Nozsa's students also read and discussed a collection of news articles about students across the country who had been denied access to classroom instruction, tickets to the prom, and opportunities to walk at graduation due to violations of oppressive dress codes.

Once Nozsa's second-grade students felt they had a strong understanding of the issue, they invited a member from the district leadership team into the classroom to hear out their concerns. In preparation for this, the class worked collaboratively to determine what they wanted to share, the examples they would use to illustrate their concerns, and what they expected to happen as a result of their meeting. Taking this meeting as a class allowed them to rely on one another to navigate what wound up being a challenging exchange – one where the district official consistently pushed back on their concerns, citing the need for "safety" in schools while explaining that some of these items could be used as weapons or to signify gang affiliation. While the immediate outcome was not what they wanted (though, the dress code *was* revised the following year in response to growing backlash from many in the community), Nozsa's students contributed to a mass effort to make their district policies more just while leaning on one another to learn what it looks and feels like to advocate for change. This experience would be key in helping them learn how to advocate, both collectively and individually, in the future.

Reason #3: "I Would Love to Do Something…But Who's Going to Listen to Me?"

Even when people know what actions they can take, too often they assume they aren't qualified to speak to the issue at hand because they aren't an "expert". Learned helplessness – the belief one won't be taken seriously and therefore are unable to shape future outcomes – is crippling to efforts to create change. One of the largest reasons those 60,000+ educators did not contact their state senators was because they felt they didn't know what to say. According to feedback from teachers, they assumed this was work best left to people who knew more or sounded "smarter" when sharing concerns. Yet, who knows more about the needs of our classrooms than the very people who work there? Of course, this fear isn't contained to only educators. People from all walks of life often feel intimidated by the idea of speaking up.

What Does This Mean for Our Teaching?

If our goal is to create a citizenry who understands they have a responsibility to make those in power understand their individual and collective needs, we need to ensure our classrooms are democratic spaces where students play a key role in shaping our curriculum and classroom practices.

For example, at the start of each school year, Chris invited his students to begin envisioning the type of classroom they want for themselves and for their classmates over the next 180 days. He began by helping them understand the rights each person possesses in the classroom (see Table 5.2) and then, over the course of the next week or so, invited his new students to determine what each person will need to do to ensure these rights are secured.

TABLE 5.2
Classroom Rights

We have the right to work and play in a safe, organized, and focused environment.

We have the right to be happy and treated with kindness and respect.

We have the right to learn new things.

We have the right to be ourselves.

We have the right to hear and be heard.

Furthermore, to make certain the classroom truly is responsive to the evolving needs of all twenty-two children, Chris then used his Morning Meeting as an opportunity to routinely check in to see how things are going. Asking questions such as *What are some things we're already doing well to make this a safe and happy classroom?*, *What could we be doing better?*, and *What's something in the classroom you wish was different, or more fair?*, he created a democratic process where his seven-, eight- and nine-year-olds played a critical role in identifying and analyzing classroom practices as well as offering solutions to any potential issues. Over the course of their school year, his students came to recognize their responsibility in maintaining a positive and productive classroom community for all.

Not Sure Where to Begin? Try This...

Supporting students to take action needn't feel daunting. There are concrete steps we can take to provide students of all ages with the knowledge, skills, and mindsets required to take actionable steps toward positive change. We will begin with a focused inquiry designed to help students see how others have taken action and then follow with specific steps you can take to scaffold students into individual or collective advocacy projects of their own.

Helping Students Learn About Advocacy and Activism

When helping students learn about advocacy and activism, we frame this inquiry around questions such as:

What is activism? What is advocacy?

Who are the people who take action?

Why do these people choose to act?

What does this look like?

What are the outcomes?

To help students conduct research aimed at answering such questions, it's helpful to create a multimodal text set consisting of picture books, chapter books, news articles, videos, and photos that feature characters, both real and fictional, taking action in communities across the globe. The complexity of the texts chosen and the amount of support offered when reading them will reflect the range of developmental needs of your particular students.

Picture Books

Due to the fact most picture books can be read in one sitting, they offer an opportunity to explore many rich examples of activism in a relatively short amount of time. Table 5.3 provides titles that feature characters of all ages working to create positive change.

TABLE 5.3

Picture Books That Feature Advocacy and Activism

Peaceful Fights for Equal Rights **by Rob Sanders**
What Do You Do with a Voice Like That? The Story of Extraordinary Congresswoman Barbara Jordan **by Chris Barton and Ekua Holmes**

TABLE 5.3 (Continued)

We Rise, We Resist, We Raise Our Voices by Wade Hudson and Cheryl Willis Hudson
The Pink Hat by Andrew Joyner
Milo's Museum by Zetta Elliott
Never Too Young: 50 Unstoppable Kids Who Made a Difference by Aileen Weintraub
Let It Shine: Stories of Black Women Freedom Fighters by Andrea Davis Pinkney
Resist: 40 Profiles of Ordinary People Who Rose Up Against Tyranny and Injustice by Veronica Chambers
Sophia Valdez Future Prez by Andrea Beaty
Emmanuel's Dream: The True Story of Emmanuel Ofosu Yeboah by Laurie Ann Thompson
Sit In: How Four Friends Stood Up by Sitting Down by Andrea Davis Pinkney
Brave Girl: Clara and the Shirtwaist Makers' Strike of 1909 by Michelle Market
Drum Girl Dream: How One Girl's Courage Changed Music by Margarita Engle
Hands Around the Library: Protecting Egypt's Treasured Books by Karen Leggett Abouraya
As Good as Anybody: Martin Luther King, Jr., and Abraham Joshua Heschel's Amazing March toward Freedom by Richard Michelson
A Sweet Smell of Roses by Angela Johnson
A Time to Act: John F. Kennedy's Big Speech by Shana Corey
Be the Change: A Grandfather Ghandi Story by Arun Ghandi and Betheny Hegedus
A Case for Loving: The Fight for Interracial Marriage by Selina Alko
Crossing Bok Chitto: A Choctaw Tale of Friendship & Freedom by Tim Tingle
Free as a Bird: The Story of Malala by Lina Maslo
Harlem's Little Blackbird: The Story of Florence Mills by Renee Watson
Her Right Foot by Dave Eggers
I Dissent: Ruth Bader Ginsberg Makes Her Mark by Debbie Levy
Martin and Mahalia: His Words, Her Song by Andrea Davis Pinkney

(Continued)

TABLE 5.3 (Continued)

My Heart Will Not Sit Down **by Mara Rockcliff**
My Two Blankets **by Irena Kobald**
Let the Children March **by Monica Clark-Robinson**
The Teacher's March: How Selma's Teachers Changed History **by Sandra Neil Wallace and Rich Wallace**
Separate is Never Equal: Sylvia Mendez and Her Family's Fight for Desegregation **by Duncan Tonatiuh**
The Youngest Marcher: The Story of Audrey Faye Hendricks, A Young Civil Rights Activist **by Cynthia Levinson**
The Power in Her Pen: The Story of Groundbreaking Journalist Ethel L. Payne **by Lesa Cline Ranson**
Pies from Nowhere: How Georgia Gilmore Sustained the Montgomery Bus Boycott **by Dee Romito**

Begin by reading aloud a small handful of these books over the course of a couple of days. After each reading is complete, invite students to analyze the story with questions such as:

What was the problem?

Who had the power to change it?

What action did they take?

What was the outcome?

Compiling answers to these questions on a class chart provides an invaluable artifact of learning that helps students begin to identify patterns across multiple stories of advocacy and activism. For instance, one theme that will emerge is that while a few people may have taken action within a particular story, almost everyone else had the power to do the same. Themes such as "We *all* have the power to create positive change", when paired with stories showing examples of this work, go a long way in helping students create new identities for themselves as potential agents of change.

For classrooms where students are capable of reading some of these texts independently, the reading and analysis can soon transition from whole group to partner work – allowing the class to collectively read, analyze, and report on each title. Another option is to allow each child to choose a book to read and

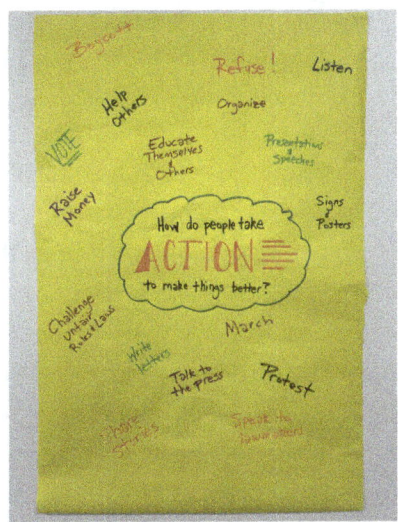

FIGURE 5.2

Class Chart Detailing Forms of Activism

analyze with a family member or caregiver. When the children return to the classroom, they report on what they learned and add it to the growing chart. This not only provides support for children who may not be ready to read such books on their own but invites family members to become an active part of the conversation. Once students have reached a point of data saturation from the book study, you can guide them to identify all the forms of activism these stories uncovered (see Figure 5.2).

Chapter Books

Chapter books can work as a powerful supplement to this study. For our youngest students, a whole class read-aloud offers students the opportunity to gain a deeper understanding of a particular change agent, as well as their motives, actions, struggles, and successes. For older students, book clubs can also be formed to offer regular opportunities to support one another through discussion.

News Articles

News articles serve as excellent non-fiction resources that help to bridge the stories found in trade books, both real and imagined, to the efforts of present-day people working to achieve necessary change – whether that be working to reduce child hunger, raising environmental awareness, or refusing to abide by unjust policies and societal expectations. Thankfully, there are news sites (such as Newsela) that cater to young audiences by adjusting vocabulary, sentence structure, and text length to help ensure more readers have access to the same information. That said, it's important to pay careful attention to what has been left out or collapsed when such changes are made.

Videos

There are many video resources available to offer students a visual representation of people engaged in advocacy and activism (such as those featured at the top of this chapter) as well as video series (such as the What Would You Do Series, available on YouTube) that show people confronting examples of unfair treatment, and sometimes outright injustice, to see whether or not they will act to protect the rights and well-being of those around them. As with all forms of text, it is important to preview potential videos to determine their relevance and appropriateness. However, when carefully selected, videos serve as powerful tools for helping students better envision the practices they are striving to grow into.

Photographs

Utilizing photographs of people engaged in advocacy provides students an important opportunity to name what they see, draw on their current experiences and understandings to infer meaning, and ask questions about those things they do not yet grasp. Displaying these photographs in the classroom and regularly referring to the discussions they elicit provides a rich resource for better understanding what it means to be an activist, what this looks like in action, and what this means to our students' growing identities as present and future agents of change.

The use of trade books, news articles, videos, and photographs is integral to helping students move from social critique (*I don't think it's right!*) to doing the work necessary to create positive change (*So, what I'm going to do is…*). These texts not only offer children a vision of what is possible but allow our students to imagine a world where they are capable of standing up and speaking out to shape a better future for themselves and their communities. Our next step is to scaffold them into this work.

Integration Is Key!

When working to scaffold classroom teachers into this work, one of the most common refrains we hear from classroom teachers is, "I'd love to be doing this work but I just don't have the time in my day". The solution to this is integration. The skills found in our state standards are the very same skills necessary to help students become more civically engaged. Additionally, integration demonstrates relevance as students see how a thread from one class, lesson, event, or discussion is woven across the days and weeks of the school year.

Reading Instruction

Whether your class is studying how to solve unknown words, implement comprehension strategies, ask and answer questions about a text, provide critical analysis, or identify the author's purpose, select activism-oriented picture books and news articles as the shared texts that fuel these studies. There are very few reading standards that cannot be taught with such texts. Integrating these texts into our reading curriculum not only supports our students' literacy learning but helps them learn more about what is going on in the world around them.

Writing Instruction

From reflective writing in response to shared texts to the posters, petitions, letters, and speeches our students' craft to inform and persuade people within the community, there are many opportunities to integrate our writing curriculum into real-world applications. Drawing on the craft lessons we already implement into our writing workshop, these authentic writing tasks allow us to teach young writers to generate ideas, write legibly, organize their writing for clarity, provide greater detail, and persuade readers. In addition, engaging them in projects that an authentic audience shapes purpose and increases engagement and interest in making the work the best possible representation of self possible.

Math Instruction

By helping us describe, analyze, and quantify emerging patterns in data, math plays a pivotal role in building a greater understanding of the social and physical worlds in which we live. When engaged in activism work, we call on students to count and calculate (such as Leah did when figuring out how much money, per student, her librarian was provided), to measure (such as one kindergarten class did when weighing the amount of classroom trash generated in week), and to create and analyze graphs and tables to identify patterns. While activism work does not primarily reside within the math workshop, the math skills our students are developing become key tools for better understanding and advocating for the change they hope to attain.

Unit of Study (Science and Social Studies)

Perhaps the most obvious pathway to integration, our science and social studies curriculum calls on students to develop basic scientific process skills such as observing, classifying, and categorizing while also developing inquiry skills such as asking appropriate questions to solve a problem, identifying cause-and-effect relationships, making connections between the past and present, using primary and secondary resources to understand events, practicing good citizenship skills, interpret and analyze data, and obtaining, evaluating, and communicating data.

Helping Students Take Action

To scaffold students into taking action individually, it's wise to first engage in whole-group advocacy projects where every child is working in response to an issue that is of interest and concern for the collective. We've seen classes launch action projects around topics such as litter, recycling, animal rights, longer recess times, and legislation for equal pay. Just as shared writing in the literacy block supports students in stronger practice and improved confidence, shared advocacy projects provide students the support they need as they begin asking critical and clarifying questions, conducting research to learn more, and executing plans of action. Students such as Ethan and Leah would have been far less likely to advocate for public education or school libraries had they not had previous experiences with shared activism alongside their classmates throughout the school year.

Advocacy projects can evolve organically in response to something students have recently learned about or experienced or can be planned in advance by their teacher. Not surprisingly, though, the most powerful and productive experiences are ones that are responsive to the particular interests, concerns, and needs of students.

In this section, we offer a structure for scaffolding students into activism. While there are many ways to successfully go about this work, this particular structure provides a straightforward approach that can be replicated for any age. This includes helping students: (1) identify issues, (2) conduct research, and (3) develop and employ plans of action. After a description of each of these below, we will offer concrete classroom examples that show how both early childhood and elementary teachers have engaged in this work alongside their students.

>   Step One: Identify the Issue
>
>   Step Two: Conduct Research
>
>   Step Three: Develop and Implement a Plan of Action

Step One: Identifying Issues That Compel Children to Act

The first step is to identify an issue the class would like to act upon. As mentioned earlier, this often happens in real time, growing directly from a recent experience around a book, a news article, a photo, etc. In these cases, students share their frustrations or concerns over an issue and the teacher responds by asking if they would like to do something to make it better. Such an approach is powerful in that it immediately captures and builds upon the emotional investment of students and demonstrates that a reasonable response to such feelings is to seek out opportunities to act.

However, for many teachers supporting students into activism for the very first time, it may feel overwhelming to act so quickly – particularly given the need to figure out how such a project will fit within their current and upcoming curricular studies. For this reason, some may feel more comfortable, at least initially, planning everything out weeks in advance to ensure they have ample time to comfortably collect resources, find connections to mandated standards, and generate learning engagements that will support students in deeper understanding and authentic action. In choosing this approach, you still want to ensure student activism grows from student concerns and interests – not your own agenda.

A great way to ensure this is to draw upon the rich classroom discussions you've facilitated throughout the year. For instance, while working to scaffold students into observing the world more carefully, questioning those things that appear unfair, and engaging in social critique, we have found it helpful to keep an anchor chart where you compile a list of the issues that have caused particular concern among your students (see Figure 5.3). Because this list has grown out of your students' experiences as well as discussions about

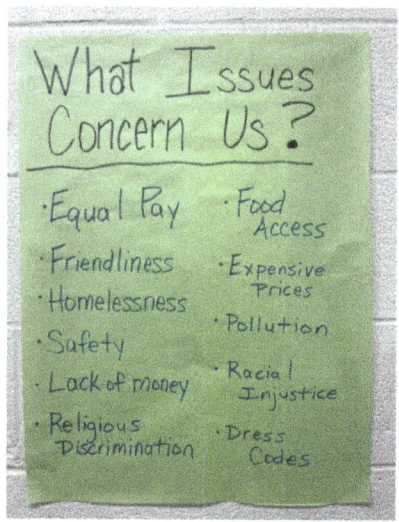

FIGURE 5.3

Anchor Chart of Issues Students Identified Throughout the Year

news articles, historical studies, and classroom literature, investment in this work is authentic in that it's responsive to students' desires and visions for more responsible and just communities.

Step Two: Conducting Research

Once you've selected an issue your students will feel compelled to address, the next step is to engage them in research. As detailed in Chapter 4, researching an issue provides students the opportunity to develop a richer, more nuanced understanding of the facts, as well as a command of expert vocabulary. This work should draw on multiple resources and, as often as possible, include opportunities to hear from those who have been directly affected. While Chapter 4 provides a methodical approach for helping students learn more about a given topic or issue, the research offered here focuses more on preparing to act. In doing so, we'll explore five key questions: (1) What, specifically, are we aiming to address?, (2) What facts will help us understand this better?, (3) What effect does this have on us and/or people within the community?, (4) What causes this to occur?, and (5) What are possible solutions?

What, Specifically, Are We Aiming to Address?

Oftentimes, issues can be quite broad. Topics such as racism, sexism, and homelessness are common conditions students would like to address; yet, these issues manifest themselves in many ways – both on the individual and systemic level. For this reason, it's important to help students define what aspect(s) of this they would like to address. While it might feel this process of refinement would better belong in the previous section on selecting your topic, we were intentional in placing it here as part of the research process because the best way to narrow down a topic is to learn more about it.

For instance, if we know our students feel strongly about the fact there are people living on the streets without a home, we can launch an inquiry into homelessness that calls on us to read a collection of picture books, chapter books, and news articles while also inviting in classroom guests who can speak to this issue with authority. As students learn more, they will soon find out there are multiple issues at play – for instance, government funding, attitudes about the homeless, and the treatment of this marginalized community. Developing a more nuanced understanding of a complex topic provides students the opportunity to begin developing greater specificity as to what it is they hope to change. In the case of homelessness, they may decide that helping others better understand, empathize with, and provide respect for the homeless is one goal; while another is to advocate for government agencies to provide greater assistance to efforts such as rapid re-housing. Of course, the age and developmental readiness of students will inform the choices they make alongside you. But engaging in meaningful research helps to ensure they are informed enough to choose wisely.

What Facts Will Help Us Understand This Better?

This aspect of research is the one that is most familiar to us – gathering facts (see Figure 5.4). Based on the age of our children, the depth of this work will vary. That said, we want to caution against underestimating our youngest students.

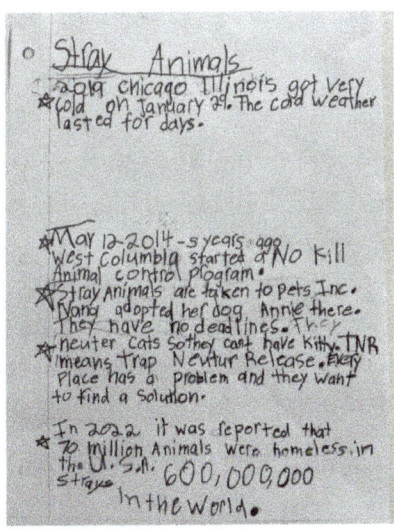

FIGURE 5.4

A Student Uses Primary Documents, Interviews, and News Articles to Collect Information About Stray Animals

Psychologist Lev Vygotsky once argued, "Children grow into the intellectual life of those around them" (1978, p. 88). This is why we offer our students the high expectations they deserve. Yes, Ethan sounded like a seven-year old when he contacted his elected officials and then reported back to his classmates about it (do you remember "Senator Ugly Suit?"), but he sounded like an informed seven year old. One of the greatest things we can help our students understand is that our goal is not simply to share our concerns and then be patted on the head and told we did a good job. The goal is to be taken seriously. The goal is to have an impact on those listening. The goal is to create change. This can only happen when we invest ourselves in research that is both developmentally appropriate and rigorous (Figure 5.4).

What Effect Does This Have on Us and/or the Community?

Once, an education lobbyist visited Chris' third-grade classroom to help his students learn how to be more effective in their efforts to inform and persuade others. Chris planned this visit to support his class' inquiry into persuasive writing, knowing it would also help his students in their advocacy work. In addition to stressing the need to have a solid handle on key facts from multiple perspectives, the lobbyist pointed out there is much power in sharing personal stories because this allows us to connect data points to the lived experiences of people in the community. For instance, if students are concerned about litter, they must be able to speak about how growing amounts of trash affect the health and happiness of those in the community – from the people who live there to the animals who live downstream. In terms of our research, this means that we must seek out resources, in all forms, that offer students the opportunity to learn about these personal stories.

What Causes This to Occur?

Next, we want students to draw on all they are learning and begin to name the root causes that underlie the actions they hope to transform. If people are littering, what are some of the reasons they choose to do so? If there are people without homes, what causes them to reach this point? If there are not enough teachers of Color in our schools, what reasons do people offer to explain this? Helping students identify the causes that underlie an issue helps them become better prepared to develop potential solutions as they work toward meaningful action.

What Are Possible Solutions to This Problem?

Lastly, we need our students to identify concrete solutions that will move the needle toward better outcomes. Table 5.4 provides examples of solutions

TABLE 5.4

Sample Student-Generated Solutions

Unsafe Conditions on the Playground	We could "… put signs up telling people to be more safe". "…tell them to stop when they're doing dangerous stuff". "…go tell the teacher". "…tell the principal what we've learned and ask her to help". "…write letters to teachers telling them ways they could help make this better".
Lack of BIPOC Representation in Historical Texts	We could "…write letters to the people who made this textbook and tell them to change it". "…write letters to other teachers so they know it's a problem. We could tell them what we've been doing so maybe they could do that too". "…make our own books about people in history and share them somehow. Maybe in the library".
Overrepresentation of Black Crime on the Local News	We could "…make our own newspaper with good stuff in it". "…ask someone from the news to come to our classroom so we could tell them to stop". "…put something about this in the newspaper the fourth graders are writing so other people know it's a problem too".

young children have identified to a number of issues in the past. However, it's crucial that your students generate solutions for their issues themselves – solutions that grow from the research they have personally conducted. As with all authentic learning, the process is often more important than the end product.

As you support your students to identify solutions, it's important to help them distinguish between treating symptoms of the problem (say, collecting school supplies for those who cannot afford them) and addressing the root causes they identified in their research (i.e. low wages, expensive school supply lists, etc.). Let's unpack this a bit to find out why.

While it's incredibly important to provide people with the resources they need to be healthy and happy, we cannot allow children to believe this is the terminal goal. Complex problems demand complex solutions. A perfect example of the oversimplification of a complex problem, and one that can be found in nearly every school district across the United States, is the annual canned food drive. Such drives are necessary because food banks most definitely need increased inventory, and not just during the winter holidays or after natural disasters. Yet, school food drives fail to address the core issues of food insecurity. They provide a temporary respite without challenging the very policies, structures, and practices that have led – and will continue to lead – families to lack the healthy food they need to meet their most basic needs. It is critical that our students come to understand the difference between treating a specific element or situation and seeking out a broader solution that has a far greater impact. When we fail to make this distinction, we run the risk of allowing them to believe "giving to the needy" helps to equal the playing field.

A second concern is how such campaigns tend to position those who are giving as well as those who are receiving. In her book, *Black Ants and Buddhists: Thinking Critically and Teaching Differently in the Primary Grades*, Mary Cowhey (2006) writes

> When kids collect canned goods for "poor people", it makes "poor people" seem like a predestined, anonymous group. It makes poverty seem like a permanent, almost genetic, condition. The children have no idea where the food goes after they drop the cans their mothers bought into the box. If we leave it at that, it is a child's imitation of an adult's token gesture of charity: tossing a coin in a beggar's cup....[This] stereotypes low-income people as passively "in need".
>
> (p. 26)

There have been many studies that have demonstrated how deeply students internalize negative stereotypes that are rooted in deficit-model thinking (Picower, 2012). We want to ensure our work in the classroom avoids positioning individuals and groups within our community (including some of our own students) in such a way. We want our students to seek out solutions that address the root causes of issues within the community while also working to build a richer, and more empathetic, understanding of those who are most affected.

Step Three: Developing and Implementing Plans of Action

Once students have conducted meaningful research, the final step is to decide what happens with this new knowledge. This is the pivotal step where we teach our students that it isn't enough to simply accumulate information and skills or to tell people how upsetting we find troubling aspects of the human condition. We must act.

As discussed earlier, a lack of agency (*I'm just one person*) and knowledge (*I wouldn't even know where to begin*) cripples many people into inaction, if not outright apathy. This is powerfully demonstrated in the 1994 film, Hotel Rwanda, during a scene where an American cameraman has moved through areas surrounding the Rwandan capital, documenting the horrific realities of the genocide being committed on ethnic Tutsis by the Hutu military. Seeing the footage, the Rwandan protagonist, Paul Rusesabagina, says "I am glad that you have shot this footage and that the world will see it. It is the only way we have a chance that people might intervene". The cameraman asks if such footage is still a good thing to show even if no one chooses to come help. Paul is shocked by this. He asks how anyone could possibly see these images and not act to help his people. Dejected, the cameraman explains, "I think if people see this footage they'll say, 'Oh my God that's horrible', and then go on eating their dinners". The scene is cynical, yet all-too-often accurate. Supporting our students into action not only helps them develop the confidence and knowledge that's needed to become agents of change; it helps them develop new identities for themselves as citizens who have a responsibility to act. Rather than continually turning back to eat their dinners, they become the ones who most often choose to engage.

Even if you don't have much personal experience with taking action, you can facilitate learning engagements with your students that will help everyone, including yourself, learn more about what is possible. As detailed earlier, one great approach is to launch an inquiry into activism early in the school year. By reading stories about people who have taken action, your class will quickly learn what options are available to them. Short of developing a full-blown inquiry, you can also help students learn what action looks like by introducing these yourself and then inviting students to help you decide which, in combination with one another, makes the most sense in light of your particular study. There are four key approaches students can take. These include (1) taking responsibility in their own personal lives, (2) increasing awareness about the issue, (3) organizing broader support, and (4) lobbying key decision-makers.

Taking Responsibility in Our Personal Lives

As much as we want our students to see their potential for creating change that targets those around them, it's essential we begin by helping them learn that all important work begins within themselves. An elementary student once captured this beautifully when asking her classmates, "Why is it when we complain about bad behaviors we always say 'they' instead of 'I' or 'we'? Because we all pretty much do it sometimes". Taking stock of our own beliefs and actions, and how these can work to maintain systems of oppression, is essential to any efforts aimed at protecting the environment, achieving greater social justice for all people, or any other effort that focuses on human behavior.

We begin by asking, "In what ways might *I/we* contribute to this problem?" It's helpful in these discussions to share our own personal stories and reflections. This serves two purposes. First, our willingness to be vulnerable and share honest stories about ourselves makes students feel safer in sharing their own. Secondly, sharing our stories shows our students that we all have times in our lives when our beliefs or actions may not have been as just or as responsible as we would have liked. They need to know that this is okay so long as we're sincerely working to do better. Contrary to the wildly false accusations that educators try to make students feel guilt or shame about who they are (particularly within discussions about race and racism), we strive to help students celebrate who they are while *also* learning that it's important to acknowledge ways we need to change to become more responsible members of our communities.

In the following vignette, Chris shares a personal reflection to invite students to share their own individual or collective practices that support the marginalization of women. This discussion is situated within a class inquiry exploring the lack of representation for women in historical texts and state standards. In their study, students have observed that few of the historical contributions of women are documented in their texts and when they are included, they're pushed to the margins – either squeezed into small call-out boxes or resigned to the final pages of a chapter.

CHRIS: So, it sounds like you feel that a big part of this problem is that some people don't think women are as good as men at certain things – the things that count as important to history, at least.

RUDY: Yeah, like people think only men do the things that are important, like being president and fighting wars and stuff.

GRETA: But women fight in wars, too.

CHRIS: Right. As you all were talking I was also thinking part of the problem might be that we're only thinking some things have been important to the history of our nation. But then we're totally ignoring all these other things that have been important as well. I know there was a time in my life when I probably would have agreed with this, that only the things men did in history were really important.

MIA: What?!

CHRIS: Well, all I ever learned about was what men had done. There was almost never anything at all about the important contributions of women. It was totally about white men and I didn't really question that, not at first. I would have never said "Men are more important" because I didn't believe that. But I also didn't question why men were the only ones in our history books. I just sort of accepted that as the way things are – because women must not have done important things too. Finally, I got a little older and started to question this. I'm wondering, are there things that happen in our classroom or in our school that support this false notion that girls aren't as good as boys or that their accomplishments aren't as important? Are there things that *we* do that somehow support this way of thinking too? Eva?

EVA: Sometimes boys laugh at each other if a girl beats one of them in a game at recess.

SETH: Hey, girls do that sometimes too. They tease the boys for losing to a girl.

EVA: Yeah, we do that sometimes.

When we are willing to acknowledge our own paths toward enlightenment, we create a classroom culture where students are more likely to adopt a growth mindset, knowing that it's okay to admit we all make mistakes on the way to knowing and doing better.

Increasing Awareness About the Issue

Beyond working to ensure their own beliefs and actions are just, another way students can take action is to work in deliberate ways to increase awareness about an issue. In doing so, they launch campaigns aimed at bringing their issues to the forefront of people's minds. Increasing awareness can begin with simple projects such as creating signs and posters. We've all seen examples of this where students create signs imploring their peers to recycle or to act with kindness. Oftentimes, though, this signage becomes little more than background noise. One way to address this is to engage your students in an analysis of posters national organizations have used to raise awareness for their own causes. A Google search such as "the most successful awareness posters" will quickly provide you with links to countless mentor texts – from historic examples like Rosie the Riveter to more recent campaigns around topics such as climate change and the power of diversity. Just as we invite young writers to my mentor texts so they can learn to notice, name, and then adopt the intentional moves writers make to help readers better understand and be moved by a text, studying exemplar awareness posters allows them to think more carefully about the use of wording, font, space, humor, graphics, pop culture, and so much more.

In addition to using signage as a means to raise awareness, students can also organize a march, a protest, or even an interactive week of awareness that invites teachers and students to participate each day by reading and discussing a carefully selected text, sharing their own experiences, and making pledges for ways they can become more involved. To exponentially expand the reach of such efforts, you can also have your students speak on the school's morning announcements or even contact a local news station to invite them in to capture what is happening. Provided the administration supports this positive attention, media coverage is a great way for students to have an impact that extends beyond the confines of their classroom and schoolhouse walls.

Organizing Broader Support

As students work to raise awareness and help educate others about their issue, they can also begin organizing support from various groups within the community. The goal here is to help peers learn how they can take concrete steps toward becoming part of the solution. We'll offer two proven platforms for achieving this. The first is to set up a table in the school where students invite their schoolmates to hear about their issue and, should they agree with what they've heard, sign a petition supporting designated solutions. They can also use these tables to help fellow students identify ways they can change their own practices to produce better outcomes. Such tables could be made available before or after school, during a lunch period, or in concert with a family night at school.

A second option is to ask your colleagues to allow a small group of students to make a formal presentation to their class. This ten-minute presentation would provide key information as well as detailed ways your students would like to see others support their efforts. In addition to recommendations about how they can alter personal practices, students may also ask their peers to join a march, talk with their families about this issue, or engage in a collaborative letter-writing campaign.

Lobbying Key Decision-makers

Our fourth and final approach to student activism is to help students directly call for change from those capable of affecting large-scale outcomes. To do this, we first need to figure out who these key decision-makers are. For instance, if students are worried about increased deforestation around their neighborhood, they need to know who has the most power to address this (say, legislators who vote on forest conservation policies or massive users of single-use such as paper or plastic cups). Often, students will assume their issues fall under the purview of the President of the United States. Such oversimplifications provide us an opportunity to build an understanding of how local and national legislative bodies, agencies, companies, non-profits, and grassroot organizations work to meet the diverse needs of our communities. If you yourself are unsure who to contact, you can always look to your students and pose the question, "Who could we ask that might know more about this so they can help us decide who to contact?" Opportunities to model that we are on this journey of learning together are invaluable in helping students come to understand we need not have all the answers to begin such work.

Once you and your students have identified who to contact, you need to determine what form of communication best fits your needs. Many will choose to write letters (see Figure 5.5). While this can be an effective means of reaching out, we suggest you also consider setting up a face-to-face meeting, whether that be physical or virtual. When appropriate, allowing our students to experience what it feels like to talk to their state senator, school board member, or newspaper editor makes them far more likely to seek these experiences out on their own later (remember Ethan asking to call legislators off the senate floor?).

Whether you choose to write, meet, or both, it's imperative to help your students make deliberate decisions about the content and delivery of the information they share. This will call on all they know (or will soon learn) about constructing a persuasive argument – whether that be in a letter, poster, brochure, speech, or multi-slide presentation.

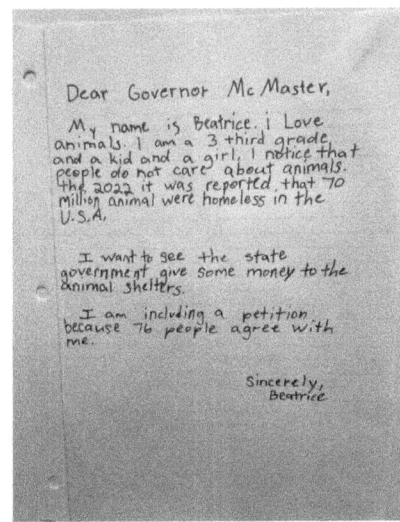

FIGURE 5.5

A Student Calls for More Funding for Animal Shelters

Classroom Examples

We will now provide a few examples showing how educators have put many of these elements into action in their own classrooms. The first example details Tiffany Palmatier's work alongside her five- and six-year-old students to address trash. The second example features work Chris did with his third-grade students, as he scaffolded them from class-based activism to developing projects addressing their own individual concerns and investments.

Kindergarteners Unite to Reduce Harmful Waste and Protect Sea Life

During an inquiry into ocean animals, Tiffany Palmatier shared a news article with her kindergarten class that featured a picture of a dead whale that had washed ashore. Her kids were immediately concerned.

DONALD: Mrs. Palmatier, what happened to that whale?

TIFFANY: Do you mean, why did it die?

DONALD: Yeah.

TIFFANY: What do you all think? What could have caused this to happen?

Positioning her students as meaning makers who would know answers to such questions, Tiffany invited the class to infer from what they saw. In response, her students drew on what they knew about life cycles and sea life to suggest possible causes. Eventually, this led them to the possibility that pollutants had entered the water.

KIARA: Sometimes animals eat trash that's in the water and get sick.

DIAMOND: Sometimes they die.

TIFFANY: Yes, you're right. That does happen sometimes.

ALEX: But how does it get in the ocean?

DONALD: Maybe people at the beach.

TIFFANY: Hmmm, that's a great question. How does this trash get into the ocean? And what types of trash is it?

Using her students' questions as a guide, Tiffany revised her plans for the unit to include opportunities to learn more about trash, pollutants, and the effects these have on aquatic animals. Over the coming weeks, they watched videos, read books, and had many discussions. Some of these focused on litter – a topic they could relate to given the amount of trash they sometimes found in the lunchroom, on the recess field, and in other parts of their community. To equip her students to take personal action, Tiffany helped them learn about the strategies of reducing, reusing, and recycling. In one of the videos they watched, they learned how people use eco-bricks, plastic containers filled tightly with trash, to build furniture and even insulate living spaces. The kids immediately wanted to create eco-bricks of their own.

Soon, Tiffany's kindergartners were bringing in empty juice containers from home and collecting trash to stuff inside. Knowing that it was important to help everyone learn about this issue, her students began circulating during lunch to tell other classes about what they were doing and to collect their trash to add to the bricks. However, after a few weeks, their motivation began to wane. Tiffany explains,

> They were so excited when we first started but after a while they started to lose their momentum. Because we couldn't use our instructional time to stuff the bricks, we had to do it during Morning Explorations when they had all sorts of other choices, like building with blocks or playing math games. After a while, there were only a couple kids left who really wanted to stuff the bricks.

Voices from the Classroom

Tiffany Palmatier, kindergarten and first-grade teacher

"The ocean pollution inquiry began with me validating the questions and concerns held by my students as they searched for the 'who' to blame for the deceased whale washed ashore. This led the children to engage in self-reflection and created a strong desire to act. Following the noticings and interests of the children positioned me as a learner, and my students had so many powerful lessons to teach me. After researching preventive efforts used by others to reduce ocean pollution, the children devised a plan focused on reducing waste and spreading awareness of the marine life casualties caused by ocean pollution. The intentionality and responsiveness displayed by the children throughout the project was a result of their investment. I could not have planned an experience as authentic and meaningful. My advice to teachers is to provide your students opportunities to lead and elevate their voices. If you do, you'll see a powerful ripple effect in your classroom, school and community".

Regardless, it remained an ongoing project that students added to when they wanted. With time, they had enough bricks to create a couple of classroom stools and then used these at an assembly where they made a formal presentation to the rest of the school about the need for reducing and reusing trash.

Another topic that emerged during their inquiry was the relationship between disposable plastic straws and the health of aquatic life, particularly endangered sea turtles. They learned that people in the United States use 500 million plastic straws per day, enough to wrap all the way around the Earth, and that some of these wound up in our waterways. Tiffany used these facts to invite her students into further action.

TIFFANY: You're right, that's a lot of straws. And out of those 500 million, some do make their way into the ocean where they hurt animals. What are some places that use the most straws, do you think?

KIARA: Kids use them a lot with Capri Suns.

TIFFANY: Right, Capri Sun! We see a lot of those in the lunchroom. Could we change this somehow, do you think?

MICHAEL: We could not use the straws and just suck it through the hole.

CLASS: [Laughter]

TIFFANY: Ha, we could Michael, you're right. But that wouldn't mean we had fewer straws. There would still be the straw from the box that winds up in the trash.

NATALIE: We could not use the straws and put them in the bricks.

TIFFANY: Yes, we could keep building more bricks to use here in the classroom. But I'm also wondering if instead of just reusing the trash, could we find a way to *reduce* how much trash we make? I'm thinking we could write a letter to Capri Sun telling them about what we're learning and suggest they find a new design for their juice packets – one that doesn't include a plastic straw at all.

ALEX: Or they could use a paper straw.

TIFFANY: Yeah, right. What do you all think?

Tiffany's students agreed and together they crafted a letter urging the company to either get rid of the straw or replace it with one made of sturdy paper. While they waited to hear back, they decided to shift their attention to nearby restaurants who also use many plastic straws on a daily basis. Tiffany's students decided each person would select a restaurant their families enjoyed visiting and write a letter to the manager. In their letters, they named the problem, shared key information, and asked for the restaurants to begin offering more environmentally friendly paper straws. Knowing her classroom parents would have different thoughts on this project, Tiffany wrote to the childrens' families about their project and invited them to keep these letters in the glove compartment so the kids could hand deliver them to the manager during their next visit. In all, eight students and their families opted to participate. These children came back and proudly shared their positive experiences with local activism.

Third Graders Develop Their Own Activism Projects

After months of scaffolding his students to think critically about the needs of their classroom and broader communities, Chris invited each of his students to identify issues that were most important to them.

CHRIS: We've done some pretty amazing things together this year. We've discussed important topics in Morning Meeting. We've read lots of books about people's lives that have helped us better understand the experiences, successes, and needs of many people. We've helped educate parents and teachers about the need for books that represent all groups of people. We've spoken with people at the State House about supporting legislation we think is important. We've worked to make our classroom more fair by questioning the way we do things and making changes when necessary. That's really important work we've done as a whole group. Today, we're going to begin a new process: We're going to start thinking about individual projects each of us could do to make the world a better place. And the first thing we'll need to do is to start thinking about what issues are most important to you, personally. What is it that *you* feel most passionately about – that *you* want to change?

Chris distributed a handout listing all the issues the class had uncovered since August, read these aloud as his students followed along, and then directed them to place a star next to the ones they felt most passionate about. Once they made their selections, Chris asked the kids to turn to a partner and explain their thinking. To set them up for success, he first modeled what this would sound like by explaining the items he had selected for himself. After everyone had an opportunity to share with a friend, the students were told to take these lists home so their families could help them narrow down their selections to a single topic they would like to research and act upon (see Figure 5.6).

After giving the kids a few days to complete this task, Chris asked his students to complete a ten-minute quick write declaring their selected topic, sharing all the information they felt they already knew about this issue, and identifying questions they would need to research. To model, Chris shared a

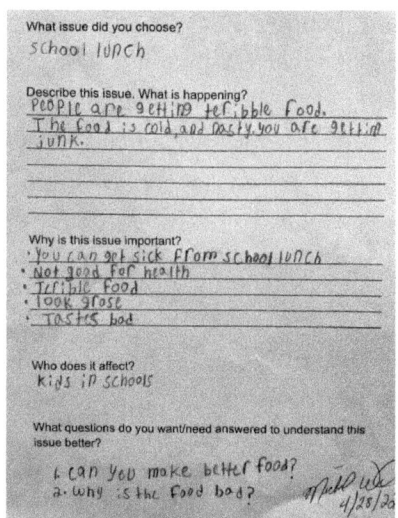

FIGURE 5.6

Student-completed Description of Their Action Project

quick write he had already completed on his chosen topic, improved school funding. These quick writes were then taken home to share with their families.

CHRIS: I want you to read what you've written to your families so they can hear what you're already thinking. Once you've read it to them, I want you to ask them to add their own paragraph just below telling you what they think *they* already know about this topic and questions *they* would want answered, as well. I'm also going to email everyone's folks to let them know they'll be helping you find some great resources to begin your research. This can be books, internet resources like websites or news articles, or even people you should interview. Our goal is to have these back in the classroom by Tuesday of next week so we can begin making plans for what comes next.

Having recorded each of the children's chosen topics, Chris used the following week to begin pulling together his own resources for the kids. He organized these by topic (litter, homelessness, playground safety, quality of school lunches, etc.) on their Google Classroom page so everyone would have easy access to the approved sites. Once they returned the forms their families helped them complete, Chris helped them conduct their own supported internet searches and added these to the links he had already posted.

Over the next two weeks, the students collected as much information as they could. People they identified as experts were asked to visit the classroom or meet via Zoom to be interviewed. During this extended research, Chris began each session with a mini-lesson where he used his own topic to model what the students' work would look like. These mini-lessons focused on topics such as: using the table of contents, using headers as a guide, identifying important information, summarizing, note taking, and responding to the text with our own thoughts and questions. Every couple days, the kids were asked to write research memos detailing key information they'd found, lingering questions they had yet to answer, and potential solutions they had already identified.

Once they felt they had reached a saturation point in their research, Chris taught the kids how to organize their data by identifying information that fit together and grouping it accordingly. Students cut sentences and paragraphs apart, glued these back together on sheets of construction paper, and then labeled them before taking them home to share. Parents and caregivers were then asked to read these over, identify any facts that needed more clarification, and help them fill in any gaps in their research. Students were also given the opportunity to meet with Chris before school or during silent reading time in case they were not able to complete this with an adult at home.

After the research was complete, Chris taught his students how to communicate what they had learned with a broader audience. They began with elevator pitches. Elevator pitches are 30-second explanations that cut to the core of the issue: what it is, what you need to know about it, and what we need to do to make it better. From here, students created a second version of their pitch that was longer and provided more detailed information. Equipped with two versions of their speeches, they wrote to classroom teachers around the school asking if they could come in and speak to their classes about what they'd been learning. The time they were provided, as well as the age of the students they spoke with, helped them decide which version of their speech to share. Each time they spoke to a class, they provided a petition students could voluntarily sign if they agreed with the proposed solutions.

Finally, the class identified who they needed to contact that would have the power to create immediate changes. Once these were identified, the students drew upon their organized notes to craft multi-paragraph letters calling for needed change. These letters went out to teachers, cafeteria managers, school administration, school board members, the mayor, the governor, and various government agencies. As is often the case, some received positive responses hinting at real change, others received form letters simply thanking them for their correspondence, and a small handful never heard back at all.

In each of these examples, we see students playing an important role in creating curriculum alongside their teachers. In doing so, these classrooms become spaces where students and teachers work hand-in-hand to make explicit

TABLE 5.5
Planning for Student Action

	Identify the Issue(s)	Conduct Research	Take Action
Tiffany Palmatier's Kindergarten Classroom	The need for activism grew directly out of a classroom experience. In this case, students saw a picture of a beached whale, showed concern, and their questions led to an inquiry into the relationship between human trash and the health of aquatic animals.	As a shared advocacy project, all books, articles, and videos were studied as a whole class. This provided Tiffany the opportunity to use these texts as an opportunity to build directly into the literacy skills her students were already learning while also helping them explore topics within both science and social studies.	Students learned to reduce, reuse, and recycle. This provided them an opportunity to collect microtrash from their homes, classroom, and cafeteria and then repurpose this into eco-bricks that were used to build classroom stools. While collecting trash in the school, they educated other students about the effects of trash and littering. They also launched a letter writing campaign to Capri Sun and restaurant managers. Some students chose to hand deliver these letters and then reported back to their classmates.

TABLE 5.5 (Continued)

	Identify the Issue(s)	Conduct Research	Take Action
Chris Hass' Third-Grade Classroom	In a unit that was developed months in advance, students were asked to draw upon issues they'd discussed throughout the school year and work alongside their families to select one they would like to research and act upon.	As an individual inquiry, Chris used his own advocacy project to model each stage for his students, often inviting them to help him with his work. Students also worked with their families to find resources they could use in the classroom. Research included books, articles, websites, and interviews. Each day began with a whole-class mini-lesson focusing on specific literacy skills that would support students while reading, writing, and speaking.	Students prepared elevator pitches and full speeches and then invited themselves into classrooms around the school to educate others. In addition, they sent letters to key decision-makers who had the most power to create immediate change.

connections between academic skills and the needs of their communities. Table 5.5 details how each of these teachers drew upon the model provided in this chapter, while also making it their own, to move their students from words to action.

Conclusion

The work that we've laid out over these past five chapters to help students build greater empathy, become aware of important issues, engage in productive dialogue, conduct critical research, and take action, is instrumental in forming the foundation for responsible citizenship. In detailing what this work can look like in early childhood and elementary classrooms, we've provided many examples from teachers and children whose efforts to use literacy as a means of creating a more just and sustainable world disprove any claims that young children just aren't old enough to understand the issues within their communities; nonetheless, create meaningful change. This work *can* be done with young children. Moreso, it *needs* to be done. But who will do it?

Without doubt, there are certain tensions that prevent many teachers from helping their students learn about issues or take action on them. In this final section, we respond to questions we often hear from teachers who have such concerns.

I'm Not Sure How I Can Help My Students Take Action on Issues Because Most of the Time I Don't Know What To Do About These Things Myself. How Can I Effectively Teach Something I've Never Done on My Own?

It's true that it's easier to teach something when we have a good amount of knowledge and personal experience from which to draw. At some point though, most of us have been tasked with teaching a topic or a skill that we don't initially feel totally comfortable with ourselves. For instance, many teachers suffered through relatively poor models of writing instruction while student in elementary school, where writing tasks focusing on formulaic practices took precedence over the authentic development of writing craft. To further complicate this, most received limited opportunities to learn how to teach writing in their teacher preparation programs. For all the emphasis placed on reading, math, science, and social studies methodologies, learning how to teach writing wasn't always given the same amount of time or focus.

Yet, what successful classroom practice has demonstrated over the past couple of decades is that inquiring into strong writing practices alongside our students is a very powerful method of learning – not just for students but for teachers as well. When we watch an interview with an author as they explain their writing process, we all become stronger writers. When we support our students to carefully study a passage from a well-written text and ask, *What is this author doing here that we could try ourselves?* we all become stronger writers. When we take a risk and put pencil to paper or fingers to keyboard every day, reflecting on what's working and what needs revision, we all become stronger writers. By inviting our students to inquire into writing alongside us, we help them learn *how* to learn – seeking out reliable sources, studying examples of what already exists, reflecting on their own practice, and so on.

The same is true with teaching advocacy. If you don't have much personal experience with taking action, dedicate yourself to learning alongside your students as you figure it out together. The inquiry described in Chapter 5, where students studied picture books about advocates and activists to learn what this looks like in practice, is a great place to begin. In addition to texts, you can also contact local non-profit organizations (say, a homeless shelter who provides transitional housing as well as career development) to help your students gain a deeper understanding of a given issue as well as to ask them to help students identify potential plans for action. By aligning student advocacy with larger efforts that are already in place, you are able to access the expertise of those who dedicate their lives to this work.

That said, some forms of action require very little – say, a letter-writing campaign or efforts to teach others what students have learned. For instance, consider these powerful, yet simple, examples from previous chapters.

Chapter 1	A fourth grader shares a piece of opinion writing with the principal about being more responsive to the needs of students with ADHD.
Chapter 2	Kindergarteners collect compostable waste from the cafeteria to reduce trash.
Chapter 3	Students across all grade levels learn to have productive discussions around sensitive topics where they challenge those around them to more carefully consider their assumptions and faulty thinking.

Chapter 4	Third graders study the lack of representation for marginalized communities of people in historical texts and write biographies they can share with the school to fill this void.
Chapter 5	Before writing a letter to the mayor, a third-grade student creates a petition to gain broader support for the homeless population.

Every form of activism and advocacy is meaningful if it creates some amount of change – whether that be affecting change in oneself, in others, or in larger institutions.

I Worry That the Kids Will Put in All This Effort to Create Change, Only to Be Let Down. What If It's All for Nothing?

It's important to acknowledge that it's possible in some cases that our students' efforts will not create immediate change. For instance, perhaps a group decides to petition the principal to extend their lunch period because after arriving at 11:13 and standing in a slow lunch line, they have to rush to eat so they can clean everything up and be out again before the next group arrives at 11:38. Chances are that if you're reading this book, you've had enough experience with lunch schedules to fully support these students' desire for a more relaxed dining experience. But to be fair, creating the lunch schedule is a complex task because there are so many children to cycle through a single lunchroom each day.

We can imagine that in this scenario, principals would fully understand and empathize with the students' needs. Yet, they're not likely to change the schedule because of all the other issues that would create, such as mid-morning and late afternoon lunchtimes. Given this, do we still support our students' efforts when they want to tackle the lunch schedule? Of course, we do. It's important to bring attention to issues, even those that don't appear to have easy solutions. Yet at the same time, we want to carefully navigate situations where someone (in this case, a principal) may thank our students for sharing and then walk away having done nothing to address their needs. When this happens, we can ask, "So, is this worth pursuing further? What might we do next?" In the case of the cafeteria, perhaps the students could propose other options for occasional dining such as an approved outdoor space or bringing lunches back to their classroom.

In supporting students when they want to take on challenging issues, we help them learn that advocacy and activism do not often provide instant gratification, and success is not always measured by getting exactly what we want. Chris' students learned this a number of years ago. After conducting a critical analysis of fairy tales to determine what sorts of messages they often convey about gender roles, the students decided to share what they learned with parents and teachers. They wanted these adults to understand the fact there are many fairy tales that promote harmful stereotypes about women so they could discuss these when they read similar titles to their children. Chris' students also decided they should share this information with a big-name book publisher. The response they received was not at all what they hoped to hear. A representative for the publisher wrote,

> Dear [Students],
>
> Thank you for your letters noting the disparity in the treatment of women in both the workplace and in fairy tales. Many of the classic fairy tales were written by the Grimm Brothers about 200 years ago when women were not recognized as equals of men. If you look at current fiction, many of the stories feature strong female characters, such as Katniss in the *Hunger Games* and Hermione in *Harry Potter*. Attitudes have changed and so have today's fairy tales.

The class was frustrated by this response. They wondered what The Hunger Games (a dystopian novel) and Harry Potter (a fantasy series) had to do with their concerns about fairy tales. They also questioned why the publisher would act as though all problematic fairy tales were written 200 years ago when they'd found a number of more recent examples and had spoken about these in their letters. They were also offended that the publisher's response acted as though their original letters hadn't acknowledged the fact that some recent fairy tales *did* do a good job of disrupting harmful stereotypes about women. Lastly, some questioned whether it was fair to say that attitudes about women had changed because the class had recently studied advertisements to see how these also supported gendered stereotypes. When Chris asked what they could do next, some wanted to let it go while others wanted to write back to argue. In the end, the class decided to shift their focus to developing questions parents, caregivers, and teachers could use to invite children into a critical reading of these texts.

We shouldn't protect our students from engaging in advocacy projects that are likely to end in varying levels of frustration. To learn to persevere, they need to know that change doesn't often come quickly or easily and that, in the face of this, it is our responsibility to bolster our efforts as we continue the fight.

I Worry About How My Administrators, Teammates, and Classroom Parents Will React. How Do I Prepare Myself for Potential Pushback?

There are a couple of reasons people may challenge the fact we're doing this work alongside our students. For one, a parent or caregiver might say, "I appreciate what you're trying to do but my child needs to be focusing on the basics". It's easy to imagine an administrator saying something very similar, questioning whether students are learning the prescribed curriculum as they venture into read-alouds and formal studies that explore empathy and issues within the community. In these cases, we have to be prepared to demonstrate how we're teaching "the basics" but are doing so within the context of authentic learning that has cultural relevance to our students' lives.

One example of this is the texts used in Chapter 1 where students learned about perspective-taking within a text while also developing cognitive empathy. Another example in Chapter 2 demonstrates how critical text sets could be implemented in three different classrooms to teach specific literacy standards. We have to be prepared to help people see that we're not making a choice between the required curriculum and efforts to support students in responsible citizenship; rather, one supports the other. Rooting literacy instruction within authentic learning experiences like researching issues, letter writing, or delivering speeches supports student engagement because the work they are doing has an authentic purpose and holds importance to their lives. At the same time, developing stronger literacy skills as readers, writers, speakers, and listeners positions students to be more successful in their efforts to learn about their communities and to create change.

The second reason some may challenge this teaching is that they work from a false belief that we are trying to brainwash students. Probably more than anything else, this is why so many teachers try to avoid politically charged topics and, when forced to confront them, try to remain "neutral" or "balanced". The desire to do so is understandable because teachers don't want to invite claims of bias or indoctrination. Yet, avoiding honest discussion of key issues is far more problematic as our silence about injustice and inequity makes us complicit in maintaining them.

Speaking to the notion of remaining neutral on key issues in his own teaching, Bigelow (1997), argues that "to pretend that I was a mere dispenser of information would be dishonest, but worse, it would imply that being a spectator is an ethical response to injustice" (p. 14). We must be mindful of what we are modeling for our students. When addressing efforts to remain balanced, Bigelow and Peterson (2002) go even further, positing that the aim of our teaching "needs to be truth rather than 'balance' – if by balance we mean giving equal credence to claims we know to be false and that, in any event, enjoy wide dispersal in the dominant culture" (p. 5). To practice responsible citizenship, students must be prepared to think critically about the issues facing their communities. This is what allows them to identify and enact meaningful solutions.

There are several steps we can take to avoid unwarranted claims of bias or indoctrination. The first is to ensure our students play a central role in creating meaning in the classroom. As detailed in Chapter 3, they do this by sharing their own questions, knowledge, experiences, and concerns in response to a classroom discussion, news article, or text. Our role is to facilitate from the side as we ask questions that position them to think more critically about a given topic.

The second step we can take is to clearly define and communicate the learning goals we have for our students that are related to civic growth. For instance, Chris and his second- and third-grade students developed the following goals for their learning and then he regularly shared pieces of these with his classroom parents and caregivers to help them better understand why teaching and learning in their child's classroom looked different than what they had likely experienced in their own schooling experiences. When sharing these goals, it's important to help families understand that we are working to help their children think more critically about the world around them as they also learn to have productive discussions with people who have diverse and unique knowledge, experiences, and perspectives to share. Another important step is to invite parents to tell us what their own goals for their children are in relation to growth as reader, writer, social scientist, scientist, community member, and citizen. When we are intentional to fold in opportunities for students and their families/caregivers to be part of the process of defining what the goals of education should be, we are better positioned to identify and implement commonalities that help us avoid inaccurate claims of indoctrination.

Learning Goals

- Appreciate the value of each person's individuality as well as the many social groups to which they belong
- Understand diversity takes on many forms and holds great value
- Possess a critical curiosity about the world

- Question social beliefs and practices
- Be informed of current events and issues affecting our communities, both near and far
- Identify acts of oppression and the false beliefs that encourage people to support these acts
- Understand the value of multiple perspectives and multiple ways of being
- Live alongside classmates and teachers in a democratic way
- Become critical consumers of information
- Take action on our convictions (Hass, 2020)

The third step we can take to avoid claims of bias and indoctrination is to ensure that the students play a key role in determining what issues they want to address – either collectively or individually. Our goal is to guide them through the process as they seek out information from as many reliable resources and direct stakeholders as possible to ensure their efforts are well-informed and do no harm. To safeguard against anyone wanting to take up a project that really can do harm, we can establish guidelines that make it clear no classroom acts of advocacy or activism should ever strip someone of their respect, civil rights, or sense of genuine belonging. For instance, we wouldn't want students making posters claiming there are imminent dangers posed by those immigrating to the U.S. whether legally or illegally. Not only would this be a misrepresentation of the truth (there are multiple studies showing illegal immigrants are arrested at half the rate of native-born U.S. citizens), but it would likely create a hostile environment for a number of fellow students and faculty members within the school.

We are grateful that you have joined us on this journey and hope that the examples from children and their teachers have informed and inspired you. We hope you have new insights and concrete steps that give you the courage to continue the journey with your students. When an issue feels overwhelming or beyond the scope of what is possible, pause a moment, breathe, and remind yourself that each small step is legitimate progress. Learn alongside your students, follow their lead, and let their passions and sense of justice be the fuel that moves the journey forward.

References

Anand, N., Sharma, M. K., Thakur, P. C., Mondal, I., Sahu, M., Singh, P., S J, A., Kande, A. S., Ms, N., & Singh, R. (2013). Doomsurfing and doomscrolling mediate psychological distress in COVID-19 lockdown: Implications for awareness of cognitive biases. *Perspectives in Psychiatric Care, 58*(1), 170–172. https://doi.org/10.1111/ppc.12803

Ashoka. (2017, February 8). *Surviving in the modern world: In conversation with Sir Ken Robinson.* https://www.ashoka.org/en-us/story/surviving-modern-world-conversation-sir-ken-robinson

Barton, C. (2018). *What do you do with a voice like that?: The story of extraordinary Congresswoman Barbara Jordan.* Beach Lane Books.

Bazalgette, P. (2017). *The empathy instinct: How to create a more civil society.* John Murray Publishers.

Bigelow, B. (1997). The human lives behind the labels: The global sweatshop, Nike, and the race to the Bottom. *Rethinking Schools, 11*(4), 1–16.

Bigelow, B., & Peterson, B. (2002). *Rethinking globalization: Teaching for justice in an unjust world.* Rethinking Schools Press.

Bishop, R. S. (1990). Mirrors, windows, and sliding glass doors. *Perspectives, 6*(3), ix–xi.

Brown, B. (2021). *Atlas of the heart: Mapping meaningful connection and the language of human experience.* Random House.

Brown, J. R., & Enos, R. D. (2021). The measurement of partisan sorting for 180 million voters. *Nature Human Behavior, 5*, 998–1008. https://doi.org/10.1038/s41562-021-01066-z

Burke, C., Harste, J., & Short, K. (1998). *Creating classrooms for authors and inquirers.* Heinemann.

Center at the University of California, Berkeley. https://greatergood.berkeley.edu/article/item/What_Happens_When_You_Tell_Your_Story_and_Tell_Mine

Center for Information & Research on Civic Learning and Engagement. (2023). *Youth are interested in political action, but lack support and opportunities.* https://circle.tufts.edu/latest-research/youth-are-interested-political-action-lack-support-and-opportunities

Cervetti, G. N., & Pearson, P. D. (2023). Disciplinary reading, action, and social change. *The Reading Teacher.* https://doi.org/10.1002/trtr.2196

Cherry-Paul, S. (2024). *Antiracist reading revolution: A framework for teaching beyond representation toward liberation.* Corwin.

Civic Mission of Schools Report. (2003). Carnegie Corporation of New York and the Center for Information and Research on Civic Learning and Engagement.

Cline-Ransome, L. (2020). *The power of her pen: The story of groundbreaking journalist Ethel L. Payne.* Simon & Schuster.

Counts, G. (1932). *Dare the school build a new social order?* Southern Illinois University Press.

Cowhey, J. (2006). *Black ants and Buddhists: Using read-alouds to connect literacy and caring conversations.* Routledge.

de Waal, F. B. M. (2008). Putting the altruism back into altruism: The evolution of empathy. *Annual Review of Psychology, 59,* 279–300.

Dewey, J. (1903). Democracy in education. *The Elementary School Teacher, 4*(4), 193–204.

Duster, M. (2022). *Ida B. Wells, Voice of truth: Educator, feminist, and anti-lynching civil rights leader.* Godwin Books.

Dupuis, J.K. & Kacer, K. (2016). *I am not a number.* Second Story Press.

Ehrenworth, M., Wolfe, P., & Todd, M. (2020). *The civically engaged classroom: Reading, writing and speaking for change.* Heinemann.

Evans, R. W., Avery, P. G., & Pederson, P. V. (2000). Taboo topics: Cultural restraint on teaching social issues. *The Clearing House, 73*(5), 295–302.

Freire, P. (2000). *Pedagogy of the oppressed.* Continuum.

Gil de Zúñiga, H., Strauss, N., & Huber, B. (2020). The proliferation of the 'news finds me' perception across societies. *International Journal of Communication, 14,* 1605–1633. https://doi.org/10.5167/uzh-228958

Giroux, H. (1988). *Teachers as intellectuals: Toward a critical pedagogy of learning.* Bergin & Garvey.

Goetz, J., Keltner, D., & Simon-Thomas, E. (2010). Compassion: An evolutionary analysis and empirical review. *Psychological Bulletin, 136*(3), 351.

Gonzalez, N., Moll, L. C., & Amanti, L. C. (2005). *Funds of knowledge.* Routledge Member of the Taylor and Francis Group.

Gould, J., Hall Jamieson, K., Levine, P., McConnell, T., & Smith, D. B. (2011). *Guardian of democracy: The civic mission of schools.* Report. Leonore Annenberg Institute for Civics of the Annenberg Public Policy Center at the University of Pennsylvania.

Gutmann, A. (1999). *Democratic education.* Princeton University Press.

Hass, C. (2020). *Social justice talk: Strategies for teaching critical awareness.* Heinemann.

Henshon, S. E. (2019). *Teaching empathy: Strategies for building emotional intelligence in today's students.* Taylor & Francis Group.

Hopkinson, D. (2021). *Carter reads the newspaper: The story of Carter G. Woodson, founder of Black History Month.* Peachtree.

Janks, H. (2014). *Doing critical literacy: Texts and activities for students and teachers.* Routledge.

Jilani, Z. (2020). *What happens when you tell your story and I tell mine? Greater good magazine: Science based insights for a meaningful life.* The Greater Good Science.

Jones, B., & Lynch, J. (2023). Teachers' and black students' views on the incorporation of African American children's literature in an after-school book club: Collaborative and culturally based learning. *Literacy, 57*(3), 209–220. https://doi.org/10.1111/lit.12326

Kay, M., & Orr, J. (2023). *We're going to keep on talking: How to lead meaningful race conversations in the elementary classroom*. Routledge.

Kelly, K., Laminack, L., & Vasquez, V. (2023). *Critical comprehension: Lessons for guiding students to deeper meaning*. Corwin.

Kelly, K., Siekman, M., & Mahan, R. (2023b). Facilitating restorative justice practices to foster conflict resolution. *The Reading Teacher, 77*(3), 418–422. https://ila.onlinelibrary.wiley.com/doi/pdf/10.1002/trtr.2247

Ladson-Billings, G. (1995). But that's just good teaching! The case for culturally relevant pedagogy. *Theory Into Practice, 34*(3), 159–165.

Laminack, L. (2018). *The king of bees*. Peachtree Publishers.

Laminack, L. (2019, July 27). *The traditional read aloud: Let's flip it!* The Robb Review. https://therobbreviewblog.com/uncategorized/read-aloud-lets-flip-it/

Laminack, L., & Kelly, K. (2019). *Reading To make a difference: Using literature to help students speak freely, think deeply, and take responsibility*. Heinemann.

Lewis, E. (2018, February 9). *What's the difference between an advocate and an activist? Have you been mislabeling?* Adobe. https://theblog.adobe.com/whats-difference-advocate-activist-mislabeling/

Levy, D. (2016). *I dissent: Ruth Bader Ginsberg makes her mark*. Simon & Schuster.

Lumbroso, V. (2015). *Empathy: The heart's intelligence* [film]. Flair Production.

Lysaker, J., & Tonge, C. (2013). Learning to understand others through relationally oriented reading. *The Reading Teacher, 66*(8), 632–641.

Lusk, A. B. & Weinberg, A. S. (1994). Discussing controversial topics in the classroom: Creating a context for learning. *Teaching Sociology, 22*(4), 301–308.

Macedo, D. (2006). *Literacies of power: What Americans are not allowed to know*. Westview Press.

Marquez, G. R., & Colby, S. R. (2021). Engaging students with culturally relevant texts: A case study of dual language learners' read-alouds. *Journal of Ethnographic & Qualitative Research, 15*(3), 205–219.

McCreary, J. J., & Marchant, G. J. (2017). Reading and empathy. *Reading Psychology, 38*, 182–202.

McKeever, B. W., McKeever, R., Choi, M., & Huang, S. (2023). From advocacy to activism: A multi-dimensional scale of communicative, collective, and combative behaviors. *Journalism & Mass Communication Quarterly, 100*(3), 569–594. https://doi.org/10.1177/10776990231161035

McParland, C. (2023, March 4). *Holy cross principal hopes book will encourage other schools to follow his lead*. Belfast Media. https://belfastmedia.com/kevin-mcarevey-philosophy-book

Mills, H. (2014). *Learning for real: Teaching content and literacy across the curriculum*. Heinemann.

Mills, H., O'Keefe, T., & Jennings, L. B. (2004). *Looking closely and listening carefully: Learning literacy through inquiry*. National Council of Teachers of English.

Mindshift. (2017, February 8). *Empathy is tough to teach, but it is one of the most important lessons.* https://www.kqed.org/mindshift/47502/empathy-is-tough-to-teach-but-is-one-of-the-most-important-life-lessons

Mirra, N. (2018). *Educating for empathy: Literacy learning and civic engagement.* Teachers College Press.

Mirra, N. (2022). *Reading, writing, & raising voices: The centrality of literacy to civic education.* National Council for Teachers of English. https://ncte.org/wp-content/uploads/2022/11/CIVICS-GUIDE-11.2.pdf

Mirra, N., & Morrell, E. (2011). Teachers as civic agents: Toward a critical democratic theory of urban teacher development. *Journal of Teacher Education, 62*(4), 408–420.

Moll, L., Amanti, C., Neff, D., & Gonzalez, N. (1992). Funds of knowledge for teaching: Using qualitative approach to connect homes and classrooms. *Theory Into Practice, 31*(2), 132–141.

Muhammad, G. (2020). *Cultivating genius.* Scholastic.

National Council for the Social Studies (NCSS). (2013). *Revitalizing civic learning in our schools. A position statement of national council for the social studies.* https://www.socialstudies.org/position-statements/revitalizing-civic-learning-our-schools#fn2

Nyong'o, L. (2019). *Sulwe.* Simon & Schuster.

Ophélie, V. (2016). (Extra)ordinary activism: Veganism and the shaping of hemeratopias. *International Journal of Sociology and Social Policy, 36*(11–12), 756–773. https://doi.org/10.1108/IJSSP-12-2015-0137

Patterson, M. M., & Bigler, R. S. (2006). Preschool children's attention to environmental messages about groups: Social categorization and the origins of intergroup bias. *Child Development, 77,* 847–860.

Pew Research Center. (2020). *Americans' news fatigue isn't going away – about two-thirds still feel worn out.* https://www.pewresearch.org/short-reads/2020/02/26/almost-seven-in-ten-americans-have-news-fatigue-more-among-republicans/.

Pew Research Center. (2020). *More than eight-in-ten Americans get news from digital devices.* https://www.pewresearch.org/short-reads/2021/01/12/more-than-eight-in-ten-americans-get-news-from-digital-devices/

Picower, B. (2012). *Practice what you teach: Social justice education in the classroom and the streets.* Routledge.

Satici, S. A., Gocet Tekin, E., Deniz, M. E., & Satici, B. (2023). Doomscrolling scale: Its association with personality traits, psychological distress, social media use, and wellbeing. *Applied Research in Quality of Life, 18*(2), 833–847. https://doi.org/10.1007/s11482-022-10110-7

Vygotsky, L. (1962). *Thought and language.* (E. Hanfmann & G. Vakar, Eds.). MIT Press.

Watson, R. (2012). *Harlem's little blackbird: The story of Florence Mills.* Random House Books for Young Readers.

Yasmin, S. (2022). *What the fact?: Finding the truth in all the noise.* Simon & Schuster Books for Young Readers.

For Product Safety Concerns and Information please contact our EU
representative GPSR@taylorandfrancis.com
Taylor & Francis Verlag GmbH, Kaufingerstraße 24, 80331 München, Germany

www.ingramcontent.com/pod-product-compliance
Lightning Source LLC
Chambersburg PA
CBHW080837230426
43665CB00021B/2870